Barry Tarshis is a free-lance writer who was born in Pittsburgh, Pennsylvania, who now lives in Westport, Connecticut, with his wife and two children, and who clings to the faint hope that someday he will be able to afford many of the indulgences described in *What It Costs*. His articles on a variety of subjects have appeared in a number of national publications, including *New York, Seventeen, Town & Country, House & Garden, Signature, Sport,* and *Travel & Leisure.* A contributing editor to *Tennis* magazine, he is the author of the recently published *Tennis and the Mind* and is the coauthor of several books with some of the game's leading players, including Rod Laver, Roy Emerson, Dennis Ralston, and Manuel Orantes.

Also by Barry Tarshis

WHAT IT COSTS
BARRY TARSHIS

Drawings by
Raymond Davidson

PENGUIN BOOKS

Penguin Books Ltd, Harmondsworth,
Middlesex, England
Penguin Books, 625 Madison Avenue,
New York, New York 10022, U.S.A.
Penguin Books Australia Ltd, Ringwood,
Victoria, Australia
Penguin Books Canada Limited, 2801 John Street,
Markham, Ontario, Canada L3R 1B4
Penguin Books (N.Z.) Ltd, 182–190 Wairau Road,
Auckland 10, New Zealand

First published in the United States of America by
G. P. Putnam's Sons 1977
First published in Canada by Longman Canada Limited 1977
Published in Penguin Books 1979

LIBRARY OF CONGRESS CATALOGING IN PUBLICATION DATA
Tarshis, Barry.
    What it costs.
    Reprint of the 1977 ed. published by Putnam, New York.
    1.   Prices—United States.   I.   Title.
[HB235.U6T37   1979]   790   78-23244
ISBN 0 14 00.5020 5

Printed in the United States of America by
Offset Paperback Mfrs., Inc., Dallas, Pennsylvania
Set in Optima

All the prices mentioned throughout *What It Costs* are
based on conversations or correspondence with the people
and organizations involved (or their representatives), as
well as on published material. Nonetheless, all the prices
are subject to change without notice, and the book in no
way obliges anyone mentioned to offer the service or
goods described at the quoted price.

This book is dedicated to the memory of my father who, along with my mother, helped to teach me the difference between price and value.

Author's Acknowledgments

It is obvious that a book of this nature could not have been written without the help and cooperation of a great number of people. The sources for much of the information I gathered are listed throughout the book, but there are many people whose names are not listed and I would like to single them out.

First of all, I'm grateful to Clyde Taylor, who shared my enthusiasm for the project when it was nothing more than a three-page outline. And I'm enormously grateful to Diane Matthews, whose own taste and sense of humor as the book's editor had much to do with the book's final form.

Martha Durham was in on the project from the start—a constant and fertile source of ideas and an incredibly thorough researcher. And Arlene Restaino's research contributions toward the end of the project were of considerable help. Among my friends and acquaintances whose ideas eventually found their way into print were Shelly Fireman, Joe Vos, Jim Grau, Dina Kaye,

Steve Rappaport, Joseph Block, Richard Kagan, and Jim Keresy. Other people who helped in one way or another include Arnold Kriss, Ronald Rothstein, Lloyd Kolmer, Mary Homi, Robert Weingarten, Tony Cabot, World Wide Divers, Inc., of New York, Steve Martin, Joe Bacal, David Wiltse, John Parsons, Bud Titsworth, Merle Debuskey, Lee Guber, Harvey Skolnick, Chuck Halper, Alan Isen, Renee Isen, Jeff Bairstow, and Nicholas Gage.

I owe a special thank-you, too, to my wife Karen and my children, Lauren and Andrew, who acted as sounding boards throughout the project.

—B.T.

CONTENTS

REDOING YOURSELF

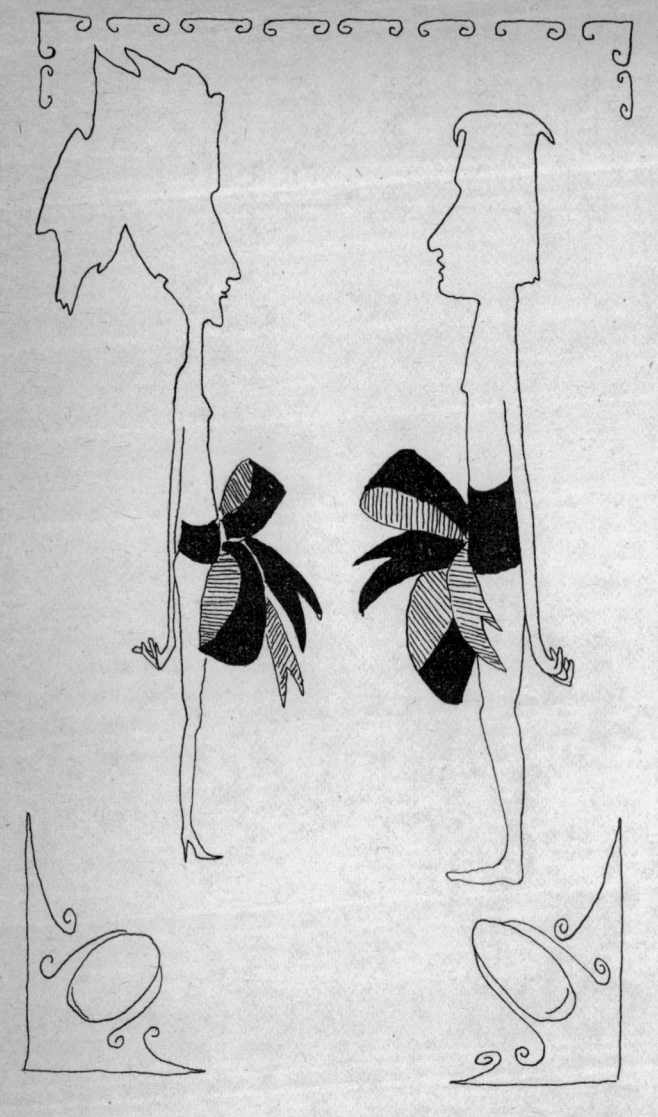

CHANGING SEXES

It all depends which way you're going. Male to female, the collective fees to the surgeon, the endocrinologist and the psychologist run in the neighborhood of $3000. Reversing the process is $15,000. Sexism? Not really. To go female to male you sometimes need as many as 15 separate operations. Most responsible sex change centers, such as the Psychohormonal Research Unit of Johns Hopkins University, in Baltimore, like you to spend at least two years living in society as a member (disguised) of the opposite sex before they perform the operation. Whether they bail you out if you get picked up for transvestism is another matter.

NICER SKIN

A technique they call dermabrasion apparently does wonders for your acne scars, your freckles (assuming you no longer want them), your birthmarks, and especially your wrinkles. Basically, what they do is sand down your skin with an electric wire brush. It's messy. You bleed and swell. Scabs form and it hurts. But once the scabs fall off, *regardez,* you have a new layer of skin. Depending on the severity of your case, it may take several sandings before your skin is entirely cleared up—if ever. And there are limits to how many treatments you can take. Base price is about $500, which buys you a clearer forehead. A full treatment on the face, at the Orentreich Medical Group in New York, ranges between $1000 and $1500.

Orentreich Medical Group
909 Fifth Ave.
New York, N.Y. 10022

A NEW NOSE

You can make it smaller, bigger, wider, narrower. You can take the bump out of it, or put a bump in it. The technical term for the procedure is a rhinoplasty. It's a major operation, but complications are rare. Your eyes stay black and blue for about two weeks. A simple rhinoplasty with a plastic surgeon who needs the money should cost around $800. Sniff carefully. Established surgeons get anywhere from $1000 to $1500. The famous Dr. Diamond, who runs a veritable factory of nose work in New York City, gets $2000, but he doesn't do anything *but* nose jobs. The hospital stay, on the average, is two days.

A FACE LIFT

It's the simplest way to take off five to ten years. Technically known as a rhytidectomy, face lifts come in a tantalizing variety of forms, but the idea in each case is pretty much the same: to tone up the saggy, loose skin from various sectors of your face. Removing the bags under your eyes—an eyebrow lift, or blepharoplasty—is a fairly simple procedure. You're in the hospital a day or so, the stitches come out in a week, and the scar is barely noticeable. A piece of cake. If you want the upper and lower parts of the eyelids lifted, figure between $800 and $1000. One or the other alone is likely to run around $500. The so-called "middle lift"—designed mainly for the skin around the cheeks—is more complicated but runs about the same price as the full eye lift. A lift aimed mainly at the sag around the neck and chin—a lower lift— is generally around $500.

If you want the works, expect a safe but major operation in which you're laid up for a week with a thick bandage wrapped around your head. It takes about two weeks before you're ready for a public showing. If the surgeon knows what he's doing, the scars will be hidden away where no one can see them (easier with women than with men). Face lifts vary enormously in price. You can probably get it done for $1500, including the eyebrow lift, but the big name plastic surgeons in New York get around $3000 or more. The Michelangelo of the face lift, Dr. Ivor Pitanguy, of Brazil, might charge you as much as $10,000, not counting the air fare. A lot has to do with how much you can afford and how much work has to be done on your face.

A STRONGER CHIN

It depends on the problem. For a chin that's too fat, a standard face lift can frequently correct the condition. Getting rid of what people call "turkey wattle"—skin that just hangs there under the skin—involves a fairly standard operation known as the "Z" process. It's painless, takes only an hour, and keeps you in the hospital a day. The problem is you can't do much talking for about a week and have to live on soup for two weeks! There is no scar to speak of, and you can get a top surgeon to do it for around $700. Dealing with a receding chin gets more complicated. It usually involves the transplanting of bone from the hip to the chin, not to mention some heavy dental work. Lots of pain. Lots of postoperative inconvenience. (Your jaw stays wired for as long as three months.) Figure at least $1500, probably more if the bone work is extensive. If you want a smaller, less protruding chin, you face major reconstructive work that will probably run close to $2500 and involve about two months of planning, casting, x-rays, etc.

SMALLER EARS

The operation, called an otoplasty, is surprisingly simple and poses virtually no threat to hearing. What's involved is the remodeling of ear cartilage, a process that rarely takes more than hour and leaves only the bare trace of a scar. The top surgeons get $800. You can get it done for $500. The hospital stay is hardly ever more than two days.

A SLIMMER REAR END

If the culprit is a generous cushion of fat within the higher regions of the buttocks, surgeons can remove it but the procedure leaves a sizable scar. Forget the St. Tropez vacation. The average surgeon will want about $1500 for the operation, which only takes a couple of hours but keeps you in the hospital for a week. If you want to dispose of those lower bulges Billie Jean King refers to as "waffles," the operation entails the removal of excess skin and fat from the waffley area and, happily, the tucking away of the scar within the crease of the seat. Also about $1500 and a week's hospital stay.

TIGHTER THIGHS

It's a simple, uncomplicated operation, but it does leave a scar. Basically, it's nothing more than the removal of excess fat and skin from the inside of the thigh. The operation lasts about four hours. There is hardly any pain, but you're in the hospital for about a week and for a good portion of that time you have to lie down with your legs elevated. The better surgeons get around $2000. Tack on another $1000 for hospital fees.

LARGER BREASTS

They call it an augmentation mammaplasty, and there are different ways of doing it. The most commonly used—and safest—method involves the implantation of a contoured silicone rubber bag filled with a gel. It has the same consistency as normal breast tissue, and you get to choose the size and sometimes even the shape. You're in the hospital about three days, and it takes about six weeks to resume your normal activities. Surgeons who do the breast enlargement operation usually charge between $1200 and $1800. Figure an additional $500 to $600 for operating rooms and lab fees. If, for some reason, you want smaller breasts, the whole process—a week in the hospital and about five weeks to recover—is between $1500 and $2000.

PRETTIER FINGERNAILS

Your problem is nails that are brittle and always breaking off, or nails that are short and stubby and not very sexy. The solution is a new development called nail extensions. Nail extensions are basically porcelain nails. On your first visit to a nail extension "center," you get an acrylic tip put on each nail. The tip is then covered with a porcelain powder that is liquefied. Your nail actually breathes through this covering, but as the nails grow out, you have to get "fill-ins" every three weeks until they've grown long enough to suit you. A fill-in is a porcelain powder application to the space between the cuticle, where the last application left off. Once the nails have become as long as you want them, you get a "cover applied"—another covering of porcelain to keep the nails stiff. The price for the whole business is around $45 for the nails (the tips plus the porcelain powder application you get on your first appointment), plus $1.50 per finger for each fill-in. The covers run around $20 and last several months. In the event a porcelain nail chips or breaks, you bring the tip in and they perform an implant, which costs $2.50. If you don't want to fool around with the acrylic, there's a process called nail sculpture that involves building up your own nail before applying the porcelain. It runs around $35. Check out the more with-it beauty salons in your area.

A VASECTOMY

Surgically speaking, a vasectomy is no more complicated than a tonsilectomy. The operation takes less than a half-hour. It is usually done in a doctor's office or clinic. A urologist with a big city practice will generally charge between $350 and $400. In smaller cities, the price can dip to $175. Many Planned Parenthood clinics perform the operation for $75. There is no charge for the little pin they give you.

A VASECTOMY UNDONE

It can be undone without any danger, but statistics show that in only about 30% of the cases have pregnancies eventually occurred. Urologists charge between $300 and $400, but no one will guarantee the results. Don't bother to consult Planned Parenthood.

A TATTOO

The superstar tattoo artists—Spider Webb, who operates out of Mt. Vernon, New York, and Lyle Tuttle, who is based in San Francisco—usually charge on a time basis. Webb gets a $25 minimum and $75 an hour for anything extensive, but he differentiates himself from the hacks at tattoo parlors, who just "put pictures on people." Tuttle, who specializes in women and has tattooed the likes of Cher Bono, Janis Joplin, Joan Baez, not to mention Flip Wilson, Peter Fonda and the Allman Brothers band, gets around the same, depending on how original you want the design and how big you want it.

If you want something modest, such as a small rose, it will probably cost you around $30. If you want the American flag across your back, it might take as much as 50 hours, so the price could well exceed $3500.

Once you get a tattoo you are entitled to membership in the Tattoo Club of America, which admits only people who've been tattooed or have contributed in some way to the art of tattooing. (Were you aware that Barry Goldwater has a tattoo and is proud of it?) The Club charges no membership fees and issues a quarterly newsletter.

Spider Webb Studios
112 W. First Ave.
Mt. Vernon, N.Y. 10550

Lyle Tuttle
30 Seventh St.
San Francisco, Cal. 94103

A TATTOO REMOVED

Assuming you don't have the map of the world across your chest, a plastic surgeon will remove a tattoo for around $300.

Oh, the range of possibilities! A week at a plush fat farm, where they smother you with luxury while limiting your calorie intake to less than 1000 per day, runs around $1000 a week for one of the top places and from $600 to $800 for the second-level places. To go somewhere and not eat anything for a week, which is to say to fast under a doctor's care, will usually run $125 for a place where you share your room with somebody else, or $300 a week where you have private accommodations. At the Dietary Behavioral Center in Miami, Florida, you can take a four-week, family-oriented program for weight control supervised by doctors from the University of Miami Medical School. Ingenious. First they limit you to a menu that has nothing on it that's fattening. Then they stick on a few fattening things just to test you. Finally, they let you go on your own to a restaurant. They also teach you how to cook without nibbling (by putting a surgical mask around your mouth), and they tell you how to stack food in a refrigerator in a way that won't invite eating. The cost is $2,240 a person for a shared room to $3,360 a person for a private suite. (For information, call 800-327-7400.) Finally, there is a theory going around that if you get a surgical staple placed in a certain part of your ear and if you wiggle that staple every time you feel the urge to eat, the urge will disappear. The theory, called staplepuncture, is vaguely related to acupuncture, and although the AMA isn't happy with it, some physicians are using the system with reasonable success. A typical staplepuncture center will charge you around $40 to put the staple in. Teaching you to wiggle your ears is presumably extra.

MORE HAIR

You have several ways to go (and grow). For a toupee, also known as a "rug" or "piece," figure a minimum of $400 for something decent—something that won't look like The Toupee from Another Planet. Hairweaving, where instead of glueing the additional hair to your scalp, they intertwine it with your own hair, runs from $450 to $700 and generally doesn't work out too well. Hair transplants—bloody and scabby and not very pleasant to go through—run around $10 to $15 a plant. If you've got quite a bit of cerebral real estate to cover, figure a good 150 to 200 plants. Then there is a new method called the Sacha-Michel process, which is sort of a combination of weaving and implanting where they take strands of hair—called wefts—and suture them to the scalp amid your normal growing hair. The actual assembly of the new hair takes a day, but it takes four to six weeks after they measure you and take samples of your hair to get it ready. If you don't want to make two trips to Encino, California, where they do it, you can do it through photographs and clippings. The cost of the process is about $2,250, plus anywhere from $375 to $500 additional for the medical fees. For people who don't live in California, there are rebates for travel charges.

The World of Sacha-Michel
16055 Ventura Boulevard, Suite 800
Encino, California 91436

A MORE DYNAMIC VOICE

Any speech coach could probably help: get you to breathe better, project more, not gulp your words as much. But so, possibly, could a six-hour session with a former opera singer and actress named Dorothy Sarnoff. Ms. Sarnoff has worked with something like 20,000 executives, government officials, authors, etcetera, most of whom came to her to learn how to come across better on radio, television and in public-speaking situations. Her promise: that with her "secret" technique, the most camera-shy person in the world will immediately lose his (or her) nervousness. Her session includes work with a closed-circuit video system. The price is $1000.

Speech Dynamics, Inc.
111 West 57th St.
New York, N.Y. 10019

A MORE PURPOSEFUL WAY OF LIFE

The best-known of a new breed of consultants known as time/planning advisers is a man named Alan Lakein, whose client list includes Polly Bergen, Abe Burrows, James Coburn, Clay Felker, Neil Diamond, Hugh O'Brian, Otto Preminger, Vidal Sassoon, Gloria Steinem, and Pauline Trigere. What Lakein does is to spend an entire day with you, during which time he tries to ascertain exactly what your goals are and whether or not your methods of achieving these goals are effective. His one-day fee for this session is $1700 (plus first-class air fare and, if necessary, hotel accommodations) but you have access to "unlimited" follow-up, which means you can call him up anytime you want or else pay him a visit if he happens to be in your city.

Alan Lakein
2918 Webster St.
San Francisco, Cal. 94123

SELF-DISCOVERY

A HOROSCOPE READING

Astrologers work on the premise that the configuration of the heavens at the moment you were born had a lot to do with the sort of personality you have and the sort of life you've lived. Also that future configurations, which can be predicted, will have a more or less predictable bearing on your future. Take it or leave it. Most legitimate astrologers do not consider themselves card-carrying fortune tellers, and do not believe that everything in life is preordained. It's just that there are periods in your life when you are more prone to misfortune. Knowing about these periods therefore, might save you a lot of grief. It takes an astrologer an hour or so to set up your basic chart, and a couple of hours from there to set up a character analysis. Some sessions can run as long as five or six hours. An astrologer with any sort of reputation is going to get from $30 to $50 for a complete reading. The astrologers who star-gaze for Hollywood stars charge from $150 for a basic reading.

A HANDWRITING ANALYSIS

The theory is that the way you write—form your letters, space them, etc.—is as valid a reflection of your personality as the way you eat, sleep, talk, and make love. People who analyze handwriting for a living are not happy when you confuse what *they* do with what the handwriting machines in airports do. One difference is price. The minimum fee for a graphoanalyst certified by the International Graphoanalysis Society is $37.50. Among the services offered by the International Graph-oanalysis Society are (1) a general graphoanalysis, in which you get a reading on the personality traits revealed in your handwriting ($40); (2) a compatibility report, which is a sort of blood test, penmanship-style—you and the person you hang out with submit your handwritings for analysis, and on that basis the graphoanalyst decides whether you should continue to hang out together ($40); and (3) a profile analysis, which is the same stuff you get in the "general" but combined with a look at what your handwriting says about your "inner" (read subconscious) desires ($100).

International Graphoanalysis Society
325 W. Jackson Blvd.
Chicago, Ill. 60606

GETTING YOUR HEAD TOGETHER

Options galore! *A TM course:* two hours a day for two days. They show you how to sit still and chant to yourself. $125. *Est:* a 60-hour marathon spread across two weekends in which people call you names, tell you when you can go to the bathroom, and stuff like that. All to help you know yourself better. About $300. *Rebirthing:* naked in a bathtub with snorkeling gear, you relive your birth. (Remember the cigars.) Around $50. *Rolfing:* massage therapy that hurts like hell because it's getting rid of a lot of calcified, built up tension. About $350 for 10 hours, with sessions mercifully spread over a week. *Primal therapy:* taking a year off to get reacquainted with primal feelings. Lots of variations. Between $2000 and $4000. *Workshops at Esalen:* the zen of jogging, the zen of tennis, the zen of sex, the zen of zen. From $30 for the weekend sessions to $300 for the week. *Biofeedback training:* a machine to tell you whether you're tense or not. It's $15 an hour for a basic machine, and around $35 an hour for something on a more sophisticated machine. *Arica:* forty days—six days a week, 10 hours a day—of exercise, dancing, meditation, chanting, interrelating, diet, and special breathing, with the whole idea to bring everything in your being into "unity." Price varies according to where you take it. Usually around $500, not including room and board. *A psychiatrist:* from $40 to $70 an hour depending on who it is. It's cheaper in San Francisco where a lot of lay therapists are shrinking heads for $15 an hour.

YOUR ROOTS TRACED

Unless you go the Alex Haley route, you'll need a genealogist—a specialist in ancestral lines. Most genealogists throughout the country charge between $25 and $50 an hour, plus expenses, but estimating the cost of specific jobs is a dodgy business. A genealogist rarely knows ahead of time how long it's going to take to dredge up the kind of information you want, especially if your ancestors were born or died in far-flung places. A routine job—ascertaining for the benefit of an exclusive colonial society that one of your ancestors did indeed come across on the *Mayflower*—should run between $250 and $300, barring a lot of travel. Getting a complete family history, a genealogy, could run as much as $50,000.

(A sidelight of interest. The Mormon Church is now in the process of assembling on microfilm as complete a record of the world's—yes, world's—genealogical records as possible, price be hanged. They have their reasons. Mormons believe in baptism not only for themselves but for all of their ancestors as well. And since Mormons are convinced that theirs is the religion of the future, they figure that someday a lot of first-generation Mormons will be hot to explore their genealogical background. Much of the information is on file already in the main Mormon library in Salt Lake City, which has more than 600 viewing machines. There is no charge for looking into the records.)

A BIORHYTHM HOROSCOPE CALCULATOR

Before you sneer, consider: an expert in horoscope biorhythms predicted that Jimmy Carter would have a lousy first debate with his predecessor but a dynamite second debate and that the Reds would sweep the Yankees in the 1976 World Series, all based on the biorhythm theory. Casio, the company that manufactures this horoscope calculator, the Biolator, makes no claims regarding the accuracy of its predictions or the validity of the biorhythm theory. The price is $29.95.

YOUR IQ TESTED (AGAIN)

Who is to say that the result of the I.Q. test given you when you were in grade school was really an accurate reflection of your intelligence and, for that matter, is still valid today? MENSA, the international high-I.Q. society, now has a take-at-home test that has been validated by whoever it is that validates I.Q. tests. They'll score it for you and send you your I.Q. in confidence. The price is $2.

MENSA
Dept. E-10
1701 W. 3rd St.
Brooklyn, N.Y. 11223

A PSYCHIC JOURNEY

There are no guarantees—certainly not for your first attempt at it. The idea is to experience what is known as an "out of body experience" (OBE). Some people call them astral flights. When it happens, your mind, in effect, "leaves" you and goes wherever you want it to go while your body stays put. Ah, the implications! You and a fellow astral tripper trysting the night together even though the two of you are 1000 miles apart. ("Dear, why are you smiling?") The ultimate implications of the OBE experience, according to the people most heavily involved, have to do with life after death—a prospect so promising that OBE training programs are gearing up throughout the country. The acknowledged leader in the field is Robert Monroe, who runs his astral travel agency out of Afton, Va. A "training" weekend runs $175, plus meals and room.

Astral Trip
Robert Monroe
P.O. Box 57
Afton, Va. 22920

FARAWAY PLACES

A TREK THROUGH THE HIMALAYAS

Alas, the Himalayas are more commercial than they used to be—people are now organizing tours designed to police up the litter—but Nepal, especially the area around the Base Camp at Mt. Everest, remains the trek of treks. You can do it in any number of ways. Mountain Travel alone has nearly a dozen different treks in and around Nepal. You can go on an eight-day introduction to Nepal trekking in which you won't go any higher than 9000 feet (around $1800, air fare included, for a 16-day trip). Or you can head for the Big E herself—the sherpa country of Khumbu at the base of Mt. Everest, a 37-day affair in which you trek for 18 days and end up at the fabled Everest Base Camp, at 18,000 feet (around $2400). Hanns Ebensten has a 25-five day trip which combines trekking to a height of 9500 feet with an elephant ride through the Terai jungle (or is it the other way around?). It runs around $2500. In each of these trips, you'll travel pretty much the way the British Raj did in the 1920's, with a support group of porters and cooks to do most of the shlepping and to take care of the chores around the camp. If such an arrangement grates on your egalitarian sensibilities, Wilderness Travel has a Nepal trek (priced from $2300 to $2500) in which the sherpas, while there to do a lot of the heavy work, function more as professionals rather than underlings. Trekking isn't the only way to go. Hemphill Harris will take you on a 54-day Himalayan expedition in which you'll be *driven* almost everywhere you go and will stay at the Everest View Hotel, if you can believe that such a place exists. It's priced at around $7500.

Hanns Ebensten Travel, Inc.
55 W. 42nd St.
New York, N.Y. 10036

Wilderness Travel, Inc.
Box 16614
Clayton, Mo. 64105

Mountain Travel
1398 Solano Ave.
Albany, Cal. 94706

Hemphill Harris Travel Corporation
10100 Santa Monica Blvd., Suite 2060
Los Angeles, Cal. 90067

TWO WEEKS IN ANTARCTICA

Better here than Philadelphia, even though the main residents on Antarctica—permanent residents, that is—are penguins and wingless flies. The weather could be better.

On some days, the temperature gets down to around −126.9°F, which isn't to mention the wind chill factor. Not that you have to worry about the cold. You're snug on the M.S. *Lindblad Explorer*. The whole trip takes a month—a week to get there, two weeks there, and a week to get back. The price, excluding air fare, is between $3600 and $4700, depending on your accommodations on board.

Lindblad Travel
133 E. 55th St.
New York, N.Y. 10022

A RIVER SAFARI IN BORNEO

The main event is a night or two spent in a Borneo "longhouse." There you get a firsthand look at a once cannibalistic communal society in which as many as 200 families live together under one roof and, fortunately, never argue about television. It's safe—they're used to tourists. If you're lucky, you get to see a birth or a wedding. The trip takes 24 days, you spend a week going down the Mahakam River, and two days on the Ujung Kulon Nature Reserve, an Indonesian wildlife sanctuary, among whose inhabitants is the one-horned Javan rhinoceros. You will have no trouble recognizing him. The safari runs around $2900. Economy fare from Los Angeles is roughly $1325.

Hanns Ebensten Travel, Inc.
55 W. 42nd St.
New York, N.Y. 10036

NEW GUINEA IN A HOUSEBOAT

It ain't the *QE II,* but it does the job. The *Sepik Explorer* sleeps 20 and meanders through around 700 miles of choice New Guinea real estate. The natives are tame, but don't expect any McDonalds or any chambers of commerce. You're on the boat for five days. The rest of the two-week trip you tour other places in New Guinea. Around $2500.

Lindblad Travel
133 E. 55th St.
New York, N.Y. 10022

A CRUISE THROUGH THE GALAPAGOS

The trip that inspired Charles Darwin to begin the research which ultimately produced *The Origin of the Species.* You're on the Equator, 600 miles west of Ecuador, in the Pacific. You cruise on a sailing yacht that sleeps 10, staying on board at night and hiking by day. You'll see sea lions and giant tortoises and iguanas and more varieties of birds and flowers than you've ever seen in your life. The trip lasts around 19 days and generally takes place in December. The cost is around $2000, not including your air fare to Ecuador.

Wilderness Travel
Box 16614
Clayton, Mo. 63105

AN INCA TREK IN PERU

On foot along the ancient Inca trail, and you don't need mountaineering experience. What you do need is a healthy pair of lungs to handle the mileage at altitudes between 7500 and 13,500 feet. You spend a lot of time in Cuzco, the capital of the Inca empire. The hotel you stay in there was once the palace of Garcilas de la Vega, one of the officers in Pizarro's army who decided to marry a nice Inca girl and settle down. It helped that she was a princess. The 16-day tour runs $1850 per person, air fare not included. Group excursion fare from New York to Cuzco through Lima is $550.

Hanns Ebensten Travel, Inc.
55 W. 42nd St.
New York, N.Y. 10036

SWITZERLAND IN A HORSE-DRAWN GYPSY CARAVAN

You mostly tour around Basel and you live, literally, like a gypsy. The caravan covers between 12 and 15 miles a day. The price for a week is $270 per person—everything but air fare included.

Swiss National Tourist Office
608 Fifth Ave.
New York, N.Y. 10020

CHINA

The China China. The original Big Red Machine. The problem isn't so much *how* much, but how you arrange it. You can't get to China without a visa and, at last look, there were about 20,000 Americans on the visa waiting list. The visa costs $6, but the Chinese are choosy about whom they give it to. You get preferential treatment if you have special skills or some area of expertise that intrigues the Chinese. Nuclear fission, say. It's easier for groups that have counterparts in China to get something going. The flight to China runs around $1850 from New York. Japan Airlines has tours that range from $1500 to $2000, air fare included.

> Sino American Club, Inc.
> P.O. Box 331
> New York, N.Y. 10022

TAHITI

If you're searching for the Tahiti that Fletcher Christian found, forgo the conventional tours, which spend too much time in Papeete, the commercialized capital. Better to charter your own yacht and sail the much more pristine outer islands: Moorea, Tahaa, Bora Bora. A Newport Beach, California, outfit called Ted Cook Tours offers a week-long sail through the Tahitian islands on a 58-foot sailing yacht called the *Danae III*. The boat has three staterooms and a salon with its own library and stereo system. It can accommodate as many as eight. You can either supply your own group or sign on as an unattached twosome (or onesome) and be part of a group arranged by the tour company. You swim, fish, snorkel, visit native villages, and play out whatever fantasies you want. Moorea, Bora Bora, Tahaa, and Huahine are the islands on your itinerary. Since the temperature in Tahiti is pretty much the same no matter when you go (between 75° to 79° on average), the trip is offered year round. The price, which includes your airfare, is based on how many people in the group. If you have six people, figure around $1300 a person. With three people, figure around $1850 a person.

AN AFRICAN SAFARI

A safari in Africa can be anything from a day-trip to a game-viewing area in a microbus to a 30-day privately escorted jaunt into the African wilderness in quest of a lion's trophy to hang over your fireplace. A simple one-day affair in which you start out at your hotel in, say, Nairobi, Kenya, and stop at a lodge like Treetops, where you can watch the wild game eating and drinking while you yourself have lunch, is around $30 a day—$40 if you stay at the lodge overnight. (Yawn!) Something a little more—well, African, in which you go into the bush for a week or so will run anywhere from $50 to $100 a day, depending on how much you want to rough it. (We're talking here about *camera* safaris in which you're led by a local guide who provides everything from the drivers to the tents to the food.) You'll pay less for the tented safaris than you will for the safaris in which you stay in well-decked-out lodges offering most of the comforts of home. On most safaris, you'll motor from place to place, but in Zambia, in central Africa, you can still take an old-style walking safari, game-viewing in either the Luangwa area or the Kafue safari trails. A seven-day trip here will run around $310 a person. A weekend visit should run around $120 a person. Work with a private outfitter—as opposed to the larger tour operators—and you figure an additional 25%.

That's for game *viewing*. If you want to hunt, it gets more complicated. First of all the number of places in Africa that will allow you to stalk big game keeps shrinking and there are limits to how much you can stalk. On a typical hunting safari in Zambia, you'll make arrangements ahead of time with a professional hunter who will meet you at the airport of Lukasa (the capital of Zambia). He'll provide the retinue of cooks, trackers, skinners, and gun bearers and will have planned an itinerary based on what you want to hunt. You choose ahead of time what you want to hunt, and you can hunt only *that* animal. Generally safaris of this nature start at around $250 a day, based on one hunter for two people. If you book for a month, figure anywhere from $8000 to $10,000, depending upon how many people in the party and how many hunters.

We're just beginning. You'll need a basic safari license. It's around $900 in Zambia and entitles you to hunt for only a limited variety of game. If you want to hunt lion, for instance, it will cost you $320 more. For the black rhino, figure $2400 extra. You pay this fee whether or not you bring back a trophy. If you want the hunter to pack, dip, and document the trophy, it's another $500. Otherwise everything is taken care of—everything, that is, except the booze (a bottle of scotch in Zambia is $18) and cigarettes ($1 a pack) and any charter fares you run up if you want to be flown directly. It costs around $1200 to fly to Zambia. There are some package safaris, camera-style, for around $1400 for a week, but for something with any real meat to it, figure $100 a day plus air fare for a camera safari.

AN AROUND-THE-WORLD CRUISE ON A FREIGHTER

You usually figure by the day, with the price running anywhere from $30 to $60, depending on how spiffy the quarters are and how romantic the stops are. Generally, when you book a freighter cruise, you pay your money well in advance, and you have to be flexible about your embarkation date. Don't ask your travel agent. Freighters don't pay commissions. The best source of information on freighter travel are the newsletters that advertise in travel magazines.

THE MOON

Sorry, Pan American, at last word, had stopped taking reservations, figuring that the 80,000 people who'd signed up would more than fill the first flight. For the record, there was no charge for the reservation. Then again, the airline was sketchy on details: no departure time, no arrival time, no word on the movie, except that it would probably be very long.

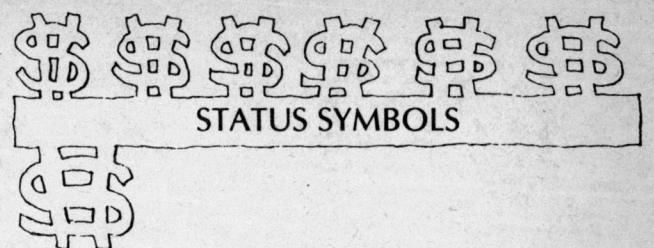

STATUS SYMBOLS

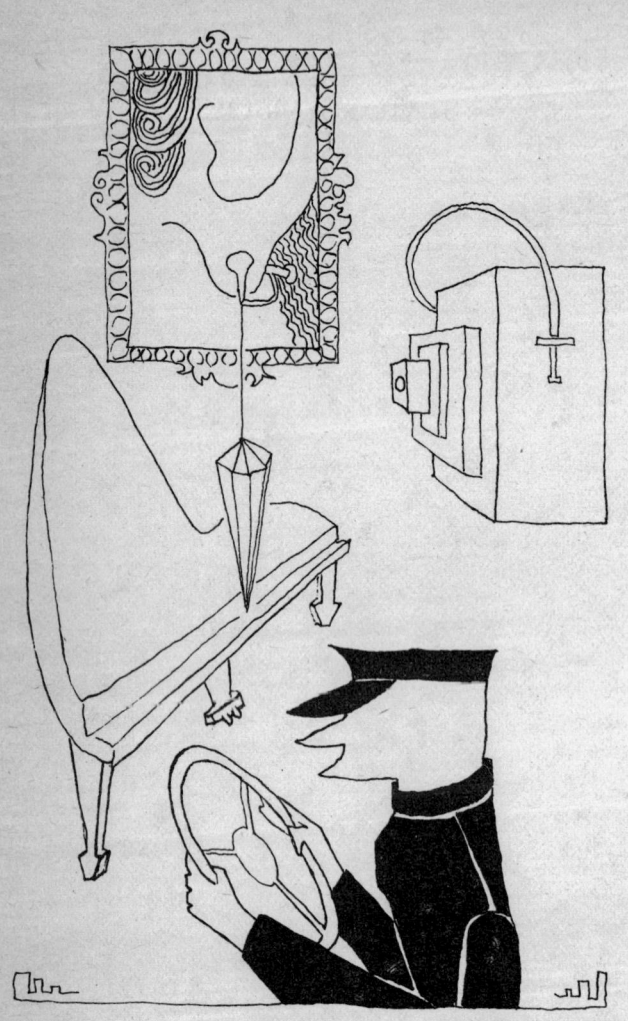

BRITISH THREADS

Let's start with a Savile Row suit. Savile Row refers to a one-square-mile area in the West End of London, only one of whose small streets is actually called Savile Row, but nearly all of whose tailors are recognized throughout the world for their peerless standards. The best known Savile Row tailoring firms are Henry Poole & Co.; H. Huntsman & Sons; Anderson and Sheppard; Kilgour, French and Stanbury; Hawkes; Donaldson, Williams and G. Ward; and Douglas Hayward. The average price for tailor-made threads in these places is $400. Huntsman gets around $650. Suits take between two and three weeks to make.

For custom shirts, see Turnbill and Asser, whose made-to-measure creations start at around $40 for cotton poplin to around $75 for silk. (Turnbill and Asser also has a ready-to-wear shirt department downstairs with prices from $20 to $30.)

Shoes? Go to Trickler's for the classic British bespoke shoe ($100). Your hat? The James Lock company, in business since 1756, will charge you $25 for the same bowler (i.e., derby) you would spend $35 for in the U.S. A sporty tweed hat should run $18 or so. To complete the picture, a Brigg umbrella from Swaine, Adeney, Brigg & Sons: in nylon, about $35; in silk, about $70.

AN ORIGINAL PICASSO FOR THE NIGHT

Or a month, or maybe even a year. What you do is rent one. Most big city museums offer lending services, with policies differing from place to place. At the Whitney Museum of American Art, in New York, simply joining the museum—$250 a year—entitles you to borrow one work from the collection for a year at no extra price except for transportation costs (anywhere from $15 to $60 one-way). For notably valuable works, there is an additional charge for insurance. The Museum of Modern Art in New York rents works of art (not from its permanent collection but from galleries around town) for 10% of the value of the work. You rent for two months with an option to buy. A Picasso etching called *L'Etreinte* will cost you $300 for two months. The $300 is deductible if you choose to buy it.

A CHAUFFEURED ROLLS-ROYCE (FOR THE NIGHT)

It's tough to arrange in Toledo but in New York, Los Angeles, San Francisco, and a few other major cities, there are limousine services that traffic in Rolls-Royces and other luxury cars. The usual fee is around $35 to $40 an hour, with most places expecting you to play the game for a minimum of three hours. If you want the car for the day, the hourly rate drops. Some places will arrange for added flourishes—Dom Perignon, beluga caviar, Sinatra music on the tape deck. If you want to just rent a Rolls with no driver, the usual price is $65 a day and 65¢ a mile. Check the *Yellow Pages* under Limousine Service.

A MINK COAT FOR THE NIGHT

From the few furriers in larger cities that have them for rent, you can figure between $60 and $75, along with a sizable deposit and some sort of indemnification, like a charge card.

A FIRST-RUN MOVIE FOR A PRIVATE SHOWING

Correction—second-run. Most of the major studios (Warner, Columbia, United Artists, etc.) have distributors who deal exclusively with the non-theatrical market. You can rent their films for a night. Usually you have to wait at least a year before the company will allow a popular film to be shown privately. Price for a top flick— *Shampoo*, for instance—is around $200, plus deposit. It comes in 16 mm.

A YOUSUF KARSH PHOTOGRAPH

Yousuf Karsh charges $1000 for one sitting. This buys you one finished print. Additional 8 × 10 inch prints cost $50 a shot. Additional 11 × 14 prints are $65 a shot. Karsh will make up a 30 × 40 portrait for $750.

Yousuf Karsh
18 E. 62nd St.
New York, N.Y. 10021

A STEINWAY

For the vertical pianos—the uprights and consoles—from $2700 to $3300 new. For the grands, from $6000 for the apartment-style 5 feet 1 inch grand to $15,000 for the concert grand. Used Steinways in good shape cost about $1000 less than the comparable new ones.

AN EAMES CHAIR

Around $1400, except that imitators are doing so well with ripoffs that some places are selling them for as little as $707.

A BETTER WATCH

The Tank watch from Cartier, originally known as "Santos," basic status, around $900. A Patek Philippe Pocket Watch (it chimes the hour, the quarter hour and the minutes, each with a different tone, and it adjusts itself for months that have 28, 30, and 31 days), around $48,000, if you want it in 18 karat gold. The Rolex Oyster perpetual day-date, 30-jewel, chronometer movement model with an 18 kt. white gold case, along with an 18 kt. white gold President bracelet, a diamond dial and diamond bezel— whatever a bezel is!— around $5,240. Higher if you want it in platinum. If you want the most expensive watch in the world, you'll probably have to get the Piaget, whose top model runs $65,000.

A BARGUZINSKY SABLE COAT

Barguzinsky sables are the best in color and quality that Russia produces. Skins on the wholesale market average around $600 each. It takes 60 to 70 skins to make a coat. For a full-length coat, figure at least $70,000.

A VICUNA COAT

Vicuna fabric, swiped from the wild, delicate animals that roam the mountains of Peru, runs around $1200 a square meter. In Paris, they sell coats for over $5000.

GUCCI LOAFERS

Around $79 for the classic, in men's and women's.

A SULKA CUSTOM SHIRT

From $70 to $125, the higher for the satin shirt. A paisley cashmere robe lined in satin with satin piping runs around $1000, and $1200 if you want it custom made. Sulka pajamas, while you're at it, run from $80 to $250.

Sulka
5 E. 55th St.
New York, N.Y. 10022

BACCARAT CRYSTAL

The difference is in the lead. That's the difference between glass and crystal. Crystal to qualify as crystal by European standards has to contain at least 24% lead oxide. Glass doesn't. Lead is what gives a piece of crystal the musical tone. Lead is what makes a piece of crystal softer and easier to cut and engrave. Baccarat is easily the most revered name in crystal, with Steuben not far behind. Their goblets in this country start at around $16 for a simple wine glass to $80 for the ornate Empire pattern. There are no discounts when you buy a complete set. Something in an oversized brandy inhaler will run anywhere from $20 to $35. A decanter suitable for a noble vintage claret will run anywhere from $75 to $175, depending on the amount of engraving. The basic Baccarat candleholder runs around $65 for one. The classic five-light candelabrum runs roughly $1250.

A DAVID WEBB ENAMEL ANIMAL BRACELET

The zebra bracelet with diamonds is as David Webb as you could want. Figure $6500. The frog runs $5500. An 18-karat gold lion cuff bracelet is $2000.

A HANDMADE BRITISH SHOTGUN

If you want the best, fly to London and check out any one of three places: James Purdey & Sons, Holland & Holland, and Churchill, Atkin, Grant & Lang. At Holland and Holland, at last glance, the basic royal game gun, in 12, 16 or 20 gauge, was ticketed at around $10,500, with the royal deluxe game gun coming in at around $16,000. Churchill gets $3500 for a simple box-lock, around $10,000 for a light-weight, side-lock game gun. Purdey's, the oldest shotgun making firm in England, asks $8000 for its least expensive model—the side-by-side gun—and $14,000 for its over-and-under shotgun. You would like game scenes or gold inlays? Can be arranged. Prices are subject to fluctuation. Delivery time is anywhere from 18 months to three years.

A PAIR OF VAN CLEEF & ARPELS RUBY
EARRINGS

The "invisible setting" jewels in which each jewel is individually set and acts as the tension that holds the other jewels in place. Around $39,000.

CUBAN CIGARS

Cuban cigars were selling, at last look, for between $2 and $2.50 a cigar, or around $50 a box.

LOUIS VUITTON LUGGAGE

For a handbag, from $75 for the smallest to around $190. A three piece set—two 26" bags and a tote—will probably run you around $800. A 24" weekender runs around $270. Steamer trunks—custom made—are around $4000. A Louis Vuitton baggage tag on its own is $5.

AN ORIENTAL RUG

Mainly it depends on how it was made—and when. You can pick up a machine-made Oriental rug—9' x 12'—for as little as $600. Something handwoven gets you into the $1500 and $2000 league. A rug that qualifies as an antique (and the way things are going in the Oriental rug market these days, a rug doesn't have to be that old to be considered an antique) is going to run you several thousand dollars at least and could be quite a bit higher. An Oriental rug that was once used to cover a pool table in a West Virginia home recently sold at auction for $200,000, not including the pool table, which is nearly twice the amount of the previous record seller. Rugs that were selling for $14,000 in 1970 are now selling for close to $40,000, mainly because a lot of oil-rich Iranians are heavily into the market.

DIAMONDS FROM TIFFANY'S

The great thing about Tiffany & Company is that the blue box they give you is the same whether it houses a bracelet that sells for $10 or one that sells for $10,000. Known mainly for their diamond jewelry, Tiffany also traffics watches, clocks, crystal, china, silver, plus a nice supply of precious-metal playthings: a sterling silver coach's whistle for $31.50; a backgammon cube for $97; a pair of 14-carat gold collar stays for $75. A Tiffany diamond ring will run you anywhere from $175 to $375,000, depending, of course, on the size and quality of the stones. Elsa Peretti's Diamonds-by-the-Yard gold chain runs around $1500. Her 18-karat gold mesh scarf will cost you $750 but won't really keep out the cold. Something in a Jean Schlumberger enamel bracelet will run you $3200. A pair of Schlumberger 18-kt. gold cufflinks with Ceylon sapphires goes for about $2300. Tiffany's line of china ranges from a $15 place setting—something in a Japanese porcelain—to the Flora Danica porcelain, which will run you $675 for a five-piece place setting and an additional $200 for each demitasse cup. Contrary to what you may have been led to believe, Tiffany's does not have a restaurant. The only way you can eat breakfast there is to do it the way Holly Golightly did—to brown-bag it and eat outside the front windows.

Tiffany
Fifth Ave. and 57th St.
New York, N.Y. 10022

SOMETHING HORSEY FROM HERMES

Hermes, a French institution since 1837, stitches together what most sages consider the greatest saddle in the world (around $1100), but they also make a tony line of scarves, ties, jewelry, watches, and accessories. A Hermes scarf—next to the saddle, scarves are Hermes' most representative item—sells for around $55. Lizard purses range from $500 to $800. A leather pochette will cost you $135, a suitcase, $400. A four-piece custom-made set of luggage goes for around $6000. Something in a beach towel with a characteristically Hermes pattern: around $70. Something in the Hermes couture line is close to $250. The Hermes silk tie runs $35. Hermes has U.S. branches in New York, Chicago, Beverly Hills, and Atlanta.

A BOSENDORFER

It's a piano. It's been made in Vienna since 1829 and it is to the Steinway what a Rolls-Royce is to a Mercedes. It takes years to build a single piano. Everything in it is handmade, and adjustments are made as the wood, metal parts, and ivory age. The reason that more concert artists don't play them is that Bosendorfer doesn't have the endorsement budget that other piano companies have. The small Bosendorfer—7'4"—sells for around $26,000. A nine-foot model goes for $35,000, and the big one—9'6"—sells for around $40,000. There is yet another European piano, the Forster, that is similar in quality and stature to the Bosendorfer, but because it is made in East Germany, it's harder to find in the U.S. It is priced somewhat higher.

Buzaid Music Company
131 West St.
Danbury, Conn. 06810

LIMOGES CHINA

Some people think that Limoges is a brand name, like Kleenex or Kellogg's or Xerox, but it's actually the name of a town in south-central France where a number of different companies design and produce lines of china. What makes the china made in Limoges special is that the undersoil in the town has something in it called kaolin, which is the main ingredient in the china originally made in China. Prices are all over the place. You can spend $45 for a five-piece setting of Limoges china and $400 for a five-piece place setting of Limoges china. You can buy a Limoges china water dish for your dog or cat for $20, or a desk set for $40. It mostly depends on the design and the detail.

BUCCELLATI SILVER

It is one thing to be born with a silver spoon in your mouth and something else again if the spoon was designed and hand-crafted by the silversmiths of Buccellati, the world's most venerated name in silver. Buccellati's flatware selection ranges from the Anacapri design, which lists for around $135 for a four-piece dinner place setting, to the Grand Imperiale line, which costs around $400 for a four-piece dinner setting. Individual serving pieces range from a silver spoon—around $31—to the Imperiale ice cream server, around $360. It's all handcrafted and marvelously balanced. Individual silver pieces vary according to design and the weight of the piece. Candlesticks run anywhere from $750 to $5000.

SHEETS FROM PORTHAULT

The theory being that you spend a third of your life in bed, anyway. A three-piece set—one sheet and two pillow cases—of Porthault bed linen with a hand-designed, hand-screened floral pattern and scalloped edges, made of 100% cotton: around $220. If you want the voile cotton (it has the texture of a fine handkerchief!) figure around $300. A set of two silk sheets and pillow cases will run about $800, but you can't get any floral patterns, only solid colors. If you want the sheets custom-sized for a 68" bed, figure about double. Porthault also makes towels ($34 for a bath towel, $12 for a hand towel, and $9 for a washcloth), down comforters (around $600). Quilted spreads start at around $600.

D. Porthault
57 E. 57th St.
New York, N.Y. 10022

THE RAYMOND DAVIDSON SKETCHES IN THIS BOOK

While they last, the originals of the Raymond Davidson sketches in this book will run you $100.

Raymond Davidson
300 E. 33rd St. Apt. 1G
New York, N.Y. 10016

PERSONAL SERVICES

A PRESS AGENT

You hire a press agent to do one of two things: get your name *into* the papers, or keep your name *out* of the papers. You can hire him on a project basis—to promote your book, restaurant, hardware store, etc.—or on a yearly basis—to promote your career. Some press agents counsel you on your public image. According to Eddie Jaffe, a savvy Broadway press agent, it was a flack named Fred Smith who persuaded Herbert Hoover to give up the celluloid collar. Another New York press agent, Sam Gutwirth, takes credit for getting Abe Beame to loosen his tie and carry his jacket for TV appearances. The general fee for any press agent who knows the ropes is around $250 a week or $1000 a month. In some cases, a press agent will take 5% of your gross up to the point at which you're grossing $5000 a week.

A WITCH

When it comes to fees for services rendered, most witches operate rather like clergymen: they don't charge you anything, but donations are accepted. Gratefully. If you insist on establishing economic guidelines, the price will depend entirely on what you want. A basic Tarot reading, which generally takes between a half-hour and an hour, should run between $10 and $20, although some of the more prosperous witches get $30 and up. A séance—and many witches won't perform them except for people they know well—usually runs from $15 to $25 a person, providing it doesn't last all night. If you want a witch to cast a spell for you, the cost will depend mostly on what sort of spell you're looking to cast. Most witches who take their craft seriously will not put the hex on anybody, since it's a basic tenet in witchcraft that whatever negative karma you lay on somebody else will come back to you threefold. A witch who doesn't believe or doesn't care about the karma business will usually charge from $25 to $50. Love potions are easier to come by but take longer. It may take several sessions over several weeks, and you should figure anywhere from $20 to $30 an hour. Be careful, though. Love spells, when they work, tend to be irreversible. A lot of witches these days have gone into psychic healing. You pay what you think you can afford. If you figure between $20 and $30 an hour, you won't get a reputation as a cheapskate. The best way to find a good witch is to talk to people who've been to several. Otherwise, check out some of the literature.

Parapsychology Institute of America
76-03 45th Ave.
Elmhurst, N.Y. 11373

A NAKED MODEL FOR A PHOTOGRAPHY SESSION

Large model agencies in most cities have a file of models willing to pose in the buff, providing you are a legitimate photographer ("Well, I own my own Brownie . . .") and are not simply looking to feed any licentious desires. The rate in the top agencies is about $500 an hour. For that you get the sort of model you might meet in the centerfold of *Penthouse* or *Playboy*. In some places, the fee is $250 an hour. You do not get a chance to interview the models ahead of time. You do the choosing through a model book.

A PROFESSIONAL ANIMAL TRAINER

Someone to make your dog or cat more civilized. Price is understandably difficult to pin down given the differences in breeds and the different needs of the owners, but the average seems to be in the $300 to $700 range, which would cover your basics: housebreaking, heeling, listening to simple commands. Training a dog to protect gets a little pricier—usually around $1500. Basic training usually lasts from two to four weeks.

AN ENGLISH BUTLER

His name won't be Hudson and he may not fulfill the expectations kindled by *Upstairs Downstairs*, but he'll be English and an experienced butler, and he'll cost you, to start, around $800 a month, plus room and board. Eventually he'll expect $1000 a month. You'll probably have to go through an employment agency that specializes in getting specialized house help. If you want someone, not necessarily a butler, to come in and serve a formal dinner, in uniform, figure around $50 for the night. Check domestic help agencies in your *Yellow Pages*.

A BIG LEAGUE POLITICAL CONSULTANT

Someone to get you elected mayor or congressman or senator or governor or maybe even president. The field of top-rank consultants isn't all that vast, and nearly all of the better known guys tend to work with candidates who wear similar political stripes. If you are a moderate to liberal Democrat, for instance, and if he liked you, you could probably get Joe Napolitan, who works out of Washington and whose campaign credits include Pat Moynihan and Jay Rockefeller, to engineer your campaign for you for around $25,000 plus all expenses. That's for the primary. For the election itself, figure another $25,000. (If either the primary or the election is a cakewalk, the price is less.) For this fee he will organize a staff, draft a budget, map out your basic strategy, and oversee your ad campaign. Unlike many consultants, Napolitan has no staff himself but knows who to hire and for how much. He won't hold your hand. On average, if you don't live in New York or Washington, he'll come to your city personally for a day or two a couple of times a month. Other people who do what Napolitan does include Sanford Weiner, of San Francisco, who engineered the successful New Jersey casino referendum in 1976; Clifford White, who managed New York Senator Jim Buckley's campaign in 1972; and Doug Bailey, who worked on the Ford campaign. Each has his own method of charging, but bottom line isn't going to be too much different from Napolitan's.

A LIE DETECTOR EXPERT

Somebody to administer a lie detector to somebody you're not so sure about. Most polygraph specialists charge by the session, which generally runs an hour. The average fee is about $30 to $40 an hour. The more successful places get $50 an hour.

A CHAUFFEUR

Full-time, using your car, figure around $200 a week as long as your hours are reasonably regular. He'll be on call whenever you need him, and when he's not driving you around, you can generally use him for errands and such. You can also rent uniformed chauffeurs part-time. The rate in most cities is between $4.50 and $6 hourly when you go through an agency. The meter doesn't start to tick until the chauffeur arrives at your front door.

AN INTERPRETER

Most interpreters work through agencies. The fee in most places is $150 a day, plus expenses. The language itself doesn't figure much in the final cost. In certain places, interpreters skilled in technical subjects get a little more. Check the *Yellow Pages*.

A VAMPIRE AUTHENTICATOR

A vampire, in case you don't know, is a living/dead person who drinks the blood of a living person in order to stay in its live/dead state. A lot of people believe in vampires, and one of them is Dr. Stephen Kaplan, the director and founder of the Vampire Research Center of America. If you suspect a vampire in your neck of the woods, Dr. Kaplan's research center will look into it for you. "We authenticate whether a vampire exists or not by investigating both primary and secondary sources," he explains. "It's not a joke. We're very serious." The charge is $500 for each suspected vampire. Somebody who is very bad at puns might call it "blood money."

Vampire Research Center of America
76-03 45th Ave.
Elmhurst, N.Y. 11373

A GHOST HUNTER

Is there really such a thing as a haunted house? The same Stephen Kaplan who authenticates vampires will send a crew and special equipment into any house you have creepy reasons to suspect is haunted. His strategy is first to eliminate any outside phenomena that might account for whatever strange happenings are giving you the willies. He and his crew will sleep at the house and will use special photographic equipment to try to capture any suspected spirits on paper. A typical ghost investigation takes from two days to a week, and the average case, according to Kaplan, runs around $500 plus expenses. In cases of economic need, he'll adjust the price.

A PERSONAL SHOPPING CONSULTANT

They're called personal shoppers and mostly they operate out of New York. Emily Cho is a prime example. She starts you out with a consultation, in which she tries to find out what sort of an image you're looking for and to what degree your present wardrobe fits that image. The consultation is $50. Ms. Cho then does some fashion reconnoitering around town on your behalf, setting the stage for the actual shopping trip she takes with you. The research is $75. The shopping trip runs $30 an hour. The whole idea is to save you time and, at the same time, as Ms. Cho explains, "to help you spend less for the look you want."

Emily Cho
663 Fifth Ave.
New York, N.Y. 10022

AN INTERIOR DECORATOR

Very open. If you work with a decorator tied into a department or furniture store, there is no fee as such, but they expect you to buy a few big-ticket items from the store. Independent decorators charge you anywhere from $20 to $50 an hour, depending upon who they are and who *you* are. In many cases, if you're using the decorator as the buying agent, the fee will be higher and the decorator will take a percentage of the price you pay for each item. Decorators who work this way point out that even with the fee you're paying them, you're saving money because of the decorator's discount. For a list of decorators who belong to the American Society of Interior Designers (not every good interior designer belongs and there are some losers in the group, but it's the official group all the same) write the Society.

American Society of Interior Designers
730 Fifth Ave.
New York, N.Y. 10019

A JAPANESE MASSEUSE WHO GIVES SHIATSU MASSAGES

Only a handful of cities, like New York and San Francisco, have them—at least those who make house calls. Figure at least $25 an hour, plus cab fare.

A BODYGUARD

Depends on where you go. Security agencies rent out armed bodyguards for anywhere from $6 to $15 an hour. The higher price fetches a guy who doesn't look like an extra from an old *The Untouchables* episode but can make like a heavy if the situation gets hairy.

A GEISHA GIRL

First of all, you have to be in Japan. Next, you have to buy not only the geisha girl but her apprentice and their musician. They sing a little, dance a little, recite a little poetry, and rap with you about world affairs. And that's it! Prices for the average geisha girl in Japan start at around $175 an hour. The meter starts the minute the

geisha girl leaves her place. It doesn't stop until she gets
back.

A CELEBRITY LECTURER

Everybody—*everybody!*—is on the lecture circuit today,
and fees are all over the place. The minimum fee for
anybody with any sort of a name is $1000, but there are
sometimes sentimental considerations—a favorite charity,
a school, etc.—that will induce a high-priced speaker to
lower his or her fee. The market is volatile. The unknown
writer you could have hired for $300 a month ago is now
getting $5000 ever since word got out that she once had
an affair with Judge Crater. At the height of the Water-
gate affair, Sam Ervin was getting $3000. You could
probably get him today for $2000. John Dean's stock—his
fee is $4000 or thereabouts—remains strong, but then
again he keeps making revelations. Network correspon-
dents of modest note—Dan Rather, Frank Reynolds, et
al.—get in the neighborhood of $2000. A heavy hitter like
Mike Wallace or Walter Cronkite will cost you $3500 or
more. William Buckley's usual fee is $3000, but he gives it
all to the *National Review*. The bidding for Jack Anderson
starts at around $6000. Truman Capote will talk about the
"beautiful" people for $3500. Rex Reed will bitch for
somewhat less.

Just about all the speakers work with bureaus, who can
supply you with a list of potential speakers and even a
subject category catalogue that runs the gamut from gay
liberation to Indian affairs to death to mysticism.

Program Corporation of America
234 N. Central Ave.
Hartsdale, N.Y. 10530

Public Affairs Lecture Bureau
109 E. 42nd St.
New York, N.Y. 10017

Keedick Lecture Bureau
475 Fifth Ave.
New York, N.Y. 10017

A MONEY MANAGER

Someone to pay all your bills, give you an allowance, stash away some savings, do some investing for you. You can work it two ways. Some firms charge a flat percentage of what you earn: from 5% to 10%, depending on how complicated your financial picture is. Other accountants and firms charge you by the hour: from $50 to $100. A person earning $100,000 with average expenses can figure someone to spend two or three hours a week working on his finances.

A MARRIAGE BROKER

Traditional marriage brokers should not be confused with new-style dating services that rely on computers and videotape machines and all the other jazz. In a typical marriage broker situation, a woman goes in for a consultation, fills out a long questionnaire, and gives the broker an idea of what she's looking for. The broker then sets up dates, sending only fellows considered suitable. Fees vary throughout the country and in some parts— New York, for instance—are limited by state law. Generally, you pay a yearly registration fee of anywhere from

$200 to $400. For this you are assured a certain number of dates a year, but no guarantees. Check the *Yellow Pages* under Marriage Brokers.

A LITERARY AGENT

Someone to take whatever you've written and try to peddle it to a magazine or book publisher. Rarely a fee. Usually 10% of whatever the work fetches.

Literary Market Place
R. R. Bowker Co.
1180 Ave. of the Americas
New York, N.Y. 10036
(Available at many public libraries)

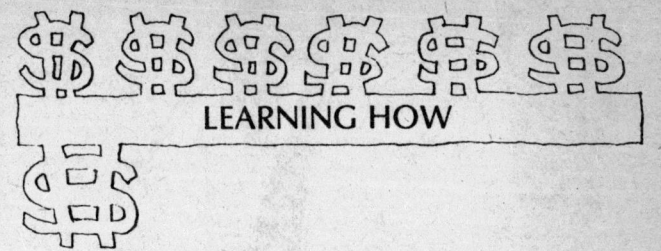

LEARNING HOW

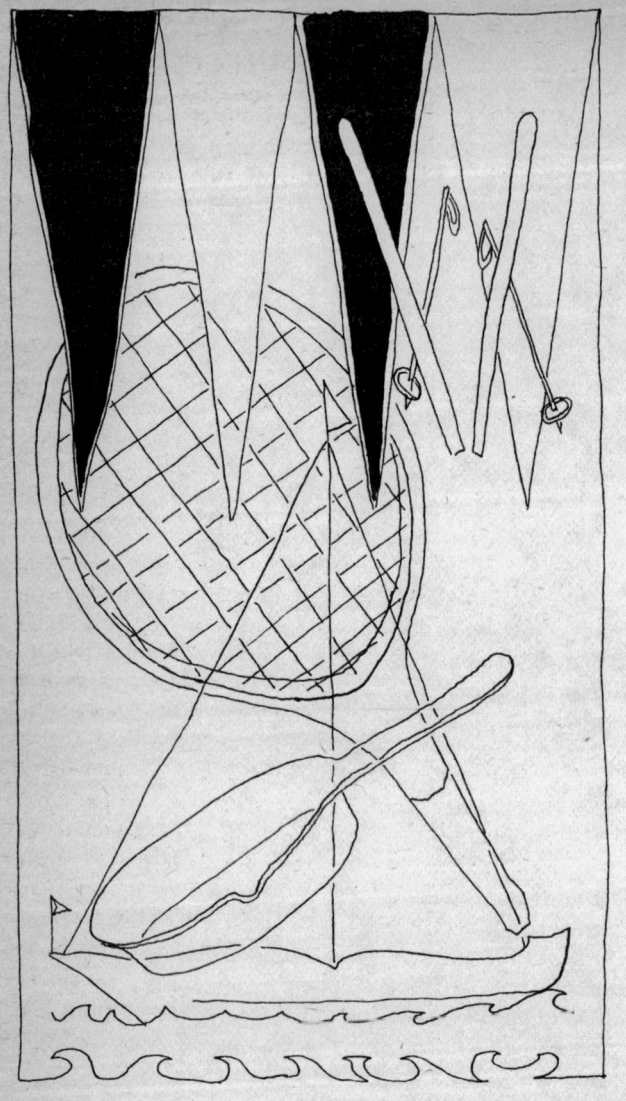

CORDON BLEU COOKING LESSONS

There is only one Cordon Bleu cooking school—it's in Paris—but there is more than one Cordon Bleu program. For $10 ($100 for a book of 12 tickets), you can attend one of the three two-hour afternoon demonstrations. You don't get a diploma, don't participate, and receive no recipes. If you're lucky, you'll get a smidgen of the partridge breasts, or whatever.

For something more official, you have four choices. A 12-week course involving two practical lessons per week and attendance at four demonstrations earns you *Le Certificat de Cuisine*. It costs $1140. A 12-week pastry course (two practical lessons and two demonstrations per week) runs $1020 and gets you *Le Certificat de Patisserie*. Pass three 12-week sessions, along with an exam, and you get *Le Diplôme del Année*. To get *Le Grand Diplôme*, you have to navigate four sessions and pass a terribly difficult oral and practical exam in which you are graded on everything, including the garnish. It will take you nearly a year and run around $4500, not to mention whatever it costs to get to and live in Paris.

A TENNIS CAMP

Anywhere from $250 to $700, depending on where you go and when. The instructional stuff at most tennis camps is generally the same: about four hours of group instruction (from four to six in each group) and drill, with some videotaping and strategy sessions thrown in, and whatever court time you can log in on your own for the rest of the day. What determines price difference is how comfortable you want to be when you're *not* on the courts. At John Gardiner's Tennis Ranch, in Scottsdale, Arizona (around $675), you stay in a smashing-looking two-room casita, get your Continental breakfast (coffee and fresh juice delivered every morning with the news-paper), eat chicken Kiev and veal bordelaise by can-dlelight, and drink vintage Bordeaux. At Don Kerbis' tennis ranch in Watervilet, Michigan (around $300), you share a dorm with about 10 other members of your sex, shower communally, and eat your meals cafeteria style. (There is, however, an open bar every night.) The best-known teaching facility in the country, Vic Braden's Tennis College in Trobúcol Canyon, Orange County, California, gets about $50 a day and this does not include your food or lodging. Dennis Van der Meer's roving program (he gives clinics at resorts and schools throughout the country) runs $195, not counting food and lodging. All American Sports, the country's largest operator of tennis camps, gets $385 for its camp program at Amherst College (the best camp for singles) and a little more than $600 at the posh Top Notch Inn in Vermont.

ITALIAN COOKING IN ITALY

Every now and then a cheery Italian-born New York cooking teacher and author named Marcella Hazan takes a small group of students—about a dozen—to Bologna, Italy, for a week of cooking, visiting places that make wine and age cheese, etc., cooking, eating in great Italian restaurants, and cooking. Marcella commandeers a restaurant for a week and that's where you do your cooking. You eat at least one of your meals at a Bolognese restaurant that offers no less than 58 first-course pastas. The cost is around $800, which includes everything but airfare.

Marcella Hazan
155 E. 76th St.
New York, N.Y. 10021

FLYING A KITE

There's more to flying a kite than meets the eye, particularly if you're talking about the kites that go for $100 or so. Will Yolen, a retired public relations executive and writer, probably knows more about kites and how to fly them than anybody in America. The author of *The Complete Book of Kites and Kite Flying* and the coach of the Yale kite team (yes, there is a Yale kite team and it's coed), he will give you a private lesson for $500, which includes the kite plus the rod and wheel. You'll need a windy day, of course. The price for arranging something like that is something else again.

Will Yolen
230 E. 44th St.
New York, N.Y. 10017

HIGH LEVEL BACKGAMMON

Backgammon isn't as hot as it was a couple of years ago, and the demand for lessons has tailed off considerably. So have fees. Accomplished backgammon players used to charge $100 an hour for a teaching session, but some will do it now for $75 or even $50. Tim Holland, the game's best known superstar and author, has a flat fee of $1500, plus expenses. This covers four hours and he doesn't care if you invite the Mormon Tabernacle Choir. Holland's spiel is designed mainly for advanced players looking to gamble for higher stakes.

Tim Holland
53 E. 66th St.
New York, N.Y. 10021

FRISBEE THROWING

Yes, fans, it's come to this: a national Frisbee organization that holds its own tournaments, has its own rankings, and is spawning its own legion of superstars who will show you how to do it for anywhere from $25 to $100 an hour. The best thing about a Frisbee lesson is that one is all you need to learn things like the overhand wrist flip. For a list of qualified Frisbee tutors in your area, write the International Frisbee Association.

International Frisbee Association
P.O. Box 664
Alhambra, Cal. 91806

THE TOTAL IMMERSION COURSE AT BERLITZ

The promise of Berlitz, the GM of the language course industry, is that two to three weeks of their "Total Immersion" course will imbue you with a "day-to-day conversational ability" of most languages you might want to learn. Total Immersion means live instruction for nine clock hours a day (there's a lunch break but you take it with an instructor), with a team of instructors who rotate like interrogators at a prison camp. You also get work to do at home, so figure an additional two or three hours a day. You can learn Spanish, French, English, German, Portuguese, and Italian—the so-called "A" languages—in five days for $950 using the Total Immersion system, or go up to as many as 30 days for $4850. There are also 10-, 15-, 20-, and 25-day courses correspondingly priced. "B" languages (all others but "A" languages) run around 5% more. You pay in advance, in any language. Check with your local Berlitz agent.

FLOWER AND PLANT ARRANGING

If you want the two top guys in New York, and maybe even the country, Roy Kohn and Bert Braff of George Cothran Flowers offer an eight-lesson course, each lesson 1½ hours, for $200. They'll condense it for you—eight hours in one day for the same price.

George Cothran Flowers
238 E. 60th St.
New York, N.Y. 10021

SKATEBOARDING

A personal lesson from Chris Chaput, one of the teenage marvels in this young but booming sport, will run you around $500 for three hours. Contact his manager, Bill Riordan.

Bill Riordan
1115 Riverside
Salisbury, Md. 21801

BRONCO RIDING

A couple of times a year, an honest-to-goodness rodeo champion name of Jim Shoulders runs a five-day clinic in bronco and bull riding. He'll supply the lunch. You make your own arrangements for board. Add insurance. About $200.

Jim Shoulders Rodeo Riding School
Henrietta, Okla. 74437

SLEEP LEARNING

It's called dormophonics and as an educational theory it's been hanging around since the latter days of World War II. The idea is to feed the subconscious mind input which it might not be as receptive to if the conscious mind were awake at the time (the conscious mind being the probable source of the various hang-ups that prevent learning). Studies in the field indicate a modicum of *some* validity to the idea, but the science is hardly exact. Still, courses are available—courses designed to help you stop smoking, stop biting your nails, lose weight, become a better salesman, bowl better, plan a better dinner party, etc.

To take a sleep-learning course, you need a specially designed tape unit. They start at $190. Adapting your existing cassette or tape recorder for dormophonics purposes will run anywhere from $25 to $70. The difference between tape units designed specifically for sleep learning and units adapted for sleep learning is that the tape units designed specifically for sleep learning can repeat the message over and over. Tapes themselves range from $5.95 to $10.

Sleep Learning Research Association
P.O. Box 24
Olympia, Wash. 98507

SURVIVING IN THE WILDERNESS

Possibly in possession of information about the future that most people don't have, a number of organizations are now offering courses in how to keep your body and soul together when it's you against the great outdoors. The best-known and most respected organization in the field is Outward Bound, which has branch schools throughout the continent and a curriculum that varies from white–water canoeing in Canada to rock climbing in California to survival camping in the Gila wilderness in New Mexico to ski mountaineering in Colorado. Prices range from $150, which buys the five-day survival camping course in New Hampshire, to $750, which covers the month-long sailing course off Hurricane Island, Maine.

Twenty-three days in the Sierra Nevadas cost $600. A 24-day bicycling trip through Nova Scotia runs $550. Room and board, such as it is, is included in the price, but not the transportation to get you to the Outward Bound launching site.

Outward Bound, Inc.
165 W. Putnam Ave.
Greenwich, Conn. 06830

POOL LESSONS FROM A SHARK

The going rate for pool lessons from an established professional player is $20, but you do it in his parlor not yours. If you want a shark to come to your place, figure $100 for three hours, plus all expenses. To find out your local neighborhood pool shark, call the nearest billiard parlor.

Professional Pool Players Association
86 Vanderbilt Ave.
Staten Island, N.Y. 10304

HIGH PERFORMANCE DRIVING

Like they do at Indy, or at any of the Grand Prix runs. According to experts in these matters, there's only one place to go: the Bob Bondurant School of High Performance Driving, near Sonoma, California. The five-day competition is the one you want. You start out in a Datsun 610 or 710 sedan. Then it's onto the racetrack in a 240, 260, or 280-Z. Graduation Day puts you behind the wheel of a Formula Ford racer. You spend a lot of time learning how to drive your way out of accident situations, and Bondurant, who was once nearly killed in a race accident, is not one to underestimate the danger element of racing. The five-day course runs $1000, with hospitalization insurance available for $5 extra a day. You can take the stunt-driving course—lots of wet and dry skids—for $250 a day.

Bob Bondurant School of High Performance
  Driving
Sears Point International Raceway
Highways 37 and 121
Sonoma, Cal. 95476

FLYING LESSONS

It used to be that flying schools figured it took 35 hours—half duo, half solo—to teach you enough to get a pilot's license. With the equipment more complicated these days (and the skies more crowded), the more reputable places figure around 50 hours. How tightly you want to cram those 50 hours is up to you. Prices range between $1200 and $1600 at most places for the entire course. Figure an additional $100 for books and ground lessons.

BELLY DANCING

From your workaday belly-dancing instructor, in a group setting, around $20 for a two-hour session. For the famous Serena, who helped put belly dancing on the map in the U.S., $100 for a private two-hour lesson.

Serena Studios
138 West 53rd St.
New York, N.Y. 10019

SKIING IN AVALANCHE CONDITIONS

Different schusses for different pusses. If you think you'd fancy skiing in stormy conditions, Sierra Avalanche Seminars will show you how to navigate avalanche terrain. They conduct seminars at various times of the year at Donner Summit, in California. Most of the instruction takes place in the field. A four-seminar package runs $125. Everything else is extra.

Sierra Avalanche Seminars
Box 8
Nordon, Cal. 95724

BETTER SEX

SEX THERAPY AT THE MASTERS AND JOHNSON CENTER

Why settle for imitations? At the Masters and Johnson Reproductive Biology Research Foundation in St. Louis, you benefit firsthand from the revelations gathered by the Center's Reproductive Biology Research Foundation. They will help you delay or accelerate your orgasm, teach you new positions, cure your impotence (or frigidity), introduce you to new erogenous zones, and who knows, maybe salvage your marriage. No singles, please: therapy is a joint affair. The typical therapy session lasts from two to three weeks and costs from $2000 to $3000, not counting your living expenses.

Reproductive Biology Research Foundation
4910 Forest Park Ave.
St. Louis, Mo. 63108

A PERMANENT ERECTION

Really! It involves an operation—the insertion into the penis of a cylindrically shaped silicone rod (custom-sized, alas) that produces, in effect, an erection that never quits. The operation is being performed mainly on men for whom no amount of conventional treatment and counseling can cure impotency.

There are complications. Like what you do with the erection when you're not using it for sex. Men who've had the operation have been relying on a jock strap device which holds the penis against the stomach. They tend to avoid public showers. A new but not yet fully mastered technique involves a prosthetic device that can be expanded and retracted at will through a tiny inflatable valve, self-activated through the penis. It's a more complicated operation that not many urologists know how to perform. The price for the basic operation averages between $400 and $700. The adaptable erection insertion runs around $1500 for the device alone. Check your urologist for the hard facts.

A TIGHTER VAGINA

You may not need it. Frequently the problem is nothing more than poor muscle tone and you can correct it by doing a series of isometric exercises called Kegel's exercises. (You contract and relax your vaginal muscles 20 to 30 times three or four times a day and hold each contraction for a few seconds.) In the event an operation is called for—and your gynecologist is the best judge—it's a minor operation, lasting a half-hour or so. You're out of sexual commission about a month. Figure between $600 and $1000.

A VISIT TO A MASSAGE PARLOR

What you spend at a massage parlor is mainly a question of how fancy a place you go to and what you have in mind apart from the massage. Most massage parlors operate as "private clubs" and clip you right away for a temporary membership fee. Figure $10. The "massage" is $15, and anything else you want is between you and your masseuse(s). If you want the girl to take off her top during the half-hour massage, figure about $5. Standard intercourse, manual sex, or oral sex (not always available) can run anywhere from $15 to $50. It's negotiable.

So much for the standard places. The superposh massage parlors—the ones with the waterbeds, the gourmet kitchens, the champagne, and the girls with Farrah Fawcett hairdos—start out with a base price of around $30. The royal works at many of these places is a champagne bubble bath in which three girls handle the ablutions. The base price is usually $100. Whatever else you want is extra. Innumerable variations play off the basic theme, but the kinkiest you're going to get are some bisexual scenes. If you just want some conversation ("I'm sorry, but I'm not that kind of girl"), it will probably cost you $25.

One nice thing about most massage parlors is that you rarely have to worry about getting roughed up or getting your wallet pilfered. Some even allow you to charge the whole thing on your American Express card (remember to get it sent to the *office*). But you have to behave. If you get drunk or ornery, they have big guys with pushed-in noses who will throw you out. Another thing. If you refuse to take off your clothes for the massage, you will probably be asked to leave. The only way cops can put the bust on massage parlor girls without running the risk of an entrapment charge is to keep their trousers on—even in the champagne bath.

A LIVE SEX SHOW

The best place to go, according to people privy to these
matters, is a seedy place in Amsterdam, Netherlands,
called Casa Rosso, where the entry fee is about $15 and
audience participation is not frowned upon. At the Chat
Noir, in Stockholm, you get a mixed bag—lesbians, male-
female—with no audience participation but in a more
comfortable atmosphere. Around $20.

A BIG-CITY CALL GIRL

Pretty much the same in most large American cities and a
little more in a few European capitals. The minimum
charge for a simple tryst—a half-hour at the most—is
usually $50, although a girl who is exceptionally attractive
may want $100. Parisian call girls start at around $75 but
that's for an hour. In Rome, you can get by for $25. In
Zurich, you may have to go as high as $150 or $200. In
most cases, the fee is for *basic* sex, which in this era of
liberation now takes in oral sex as well. Kinkier scenes are
listed below. If you're interested in a somewhat longer-
term relationship—say, the evening—the price goes up
correspondingly: figure $200 at least for a top-drawer girl.
High-ticket girls in New York get as much as $1000 for an
entire day. The majority of their customers are oil-rich
Arabs.

KINKY SEX

The big question, of course, is just how kinky you want
to get. The general rule is, the more esoteric your
appetites, the more limited the available market and the

higher the price. Costs, though, tend to be relative: according to the price structure in your city and according to what the seller normally charges. The pricing ground rules in the following situation involve a girl who expects about $50 for a half-hour for basic sex.

Slave and Master. The general procedure is that *you* play the slave, and the girl's job is to humiliate you as best she can. As long as you don't want to be *physically* hurt, you shouldn't have much trouble finding a girl to act out the part. One of the most familiar variations on the slave/master theme is for you to go to the girl's place, clean up for her, cook a meal and all the while have her abusively remind you that you are possibly the vilest, creepiest, dumbest human being on the face of the earth. Costuming is possible but not necessary to the charade. Girls experienced at this sort of thing will insist that you crawl on all fours and lick their shoes, but not all of them are convincing. Try and get somebody who's been to acting school. If there's no sex involved, just humiliation, figure $100 for an hour.

Basic Sado-Masochism. The same basic guidelines. The more pain you wish to receive—the harder you want to be whipped, paddled or spanked—the more expensive it's going to get. Most call girls draw the line at anything that will draw blood. If you want a very bloody scene, you'll have to shop around and it could cost you upwards of $500. Simple paddling and spanking without the sex will probably run about $150. Something with whips and costumes gets you into the $200 category.

Fetishism. Hard to figure. Something reasonably palatable, involving, say, the armpit, shouldn't cost you any more than $75 for a short session. If you want to hide all the girl's clothing and have her search naked for them while you issue clues, figure $100. If you want to give the girl a pedicure, figure $75, or $50 if you give a very good one.

93

Voyeurism. Again, lots of possibilities. A girl to undress while you peek through a keyhole: $50. A girl to use a dildo or vibrator: $100. Two girls making it together while you watch: around $150. (Figure $50 more if you want one of the girls to service you when she's finished.) *Three* girls making it while you watch: $225. A guy and a girl: $100 for the guy; $150 for the girl.

Miscellany. A short tryst late at night at a cemetery: about $200, if you can find the girl. Anything involving animals: a minimum of $500 and you have to do a lot of shopping around. A girl to tell you dirty stories while you masturbate: around $75 for a girl who's a gifted story-teller. A girl who will let *you* inflict pain. Very tough to find and no set pricing guidelines.

STAGING AN ORGY

Basically it comes down to numbers and time: how many girls for how long and, most important, how many buyers. A good base figure is $100 an hour for each girl based on a one-girl-to-one-guy ratio. This is providing you don't want anything too kinky. If there are more girls than guys, the price stays the same. If there are *less* girls than guys, you pay extra for each additional john. (You can usually work out some pro-rated basis.) The safest way to go about the whole thing is to leave it up to a savvy madam to make all the arrangements. She'll take care of the food and booze and even set up the place for you—at normal catering prices. All payments in advance, please.

A LIBRARY OF PORNO MOVIES

Hard-core porno movies run anywhere from $20 for a clumsily made 10 to 15 minute short to as much as $500 or so for something you could get by with calling "art." If you want to rent a name porno flick, like *Deep Throat*, figure at least $250 when they're available—more around the holidays. Your local porn shop is the best source.

A GIGOLO

Most gigolos freelance and work on a referral basis. You get the name of one from a friend who has used him and you call. Price is rarely discussed. Usually, it's a full night on the town, with you picking up the tab for the dinner, the play, etc. Payment can take the form of either a very nice gift—something worth well in excess of $100—or straight cash. Figure $100 for somebody with a lot of class. If you don't intend to call upon the guy again, $50 should suffice.

HOME IMPROVEMENTS

A MORE WORKABLE KITCHEN

It begins with the right ambience. French terra cotta floor tiles—around $750 for a 9 × 12 foot room—and Portuguese tiles to add sex appeal to the space behind the range and sink. Figure at least $250. You'll want a Sub Zero stainless steel paneled refrigerator built into the wall (the reason you build it in is to make it flush with the counters). Together with an adjacent freezer (you get 3200 cubic feet) figure $1450, which includes an ice maker. You'll want a restaurant-style range with at least eight burners, a deep fat fryer, and a charbroiler, along with a built-in double wall oven that has a microwave oven and a stay-hot oven. Figure $1600. To deal with garbage, you'll want the Kitchen Aid Trash compactor (around $380), along with a disposal unit ($170 or so). The Kitchen Aid dishwasher should run around $400.

A sink? Elkay makes a stainless steel triple sink with chrome-on-brass faucets mounted on a white ceramic deck. The center sink has a garbage disposal. The other two have pop up drains. It costs $770, but you can get an instant hot water dispenser for an additional $100 and a water cooler unit for an extra $335. A lotion or soap dispenser is available, too—for $27.

So much for the basics. A soda fountain, complete with compressor, carbonator, a full set of jars and pumps for syrups and toppings, etc., along with a capacity for 18 gallons of ice cream, shouldn't run you more than $3500. The Cuisinart Food Processor runs around $225. A really good mixer, like the Kitchen Aid K5A is $240. Pots and pans? Pick the Cuisinart stainless steel line with bottoms of quarter-inch rolled aluminum. The 1½ quart saucepan runs $27 ($8 for the lid). The 8½ quart stockpot runs $77. Figure $300 for the works. Add $150 or so for incidentals, like an omelet pan and a wok.

A NICER BATHROOM

Your main expense will involve the floor and the walls. An onyx floor inlaid with precious stones should run you no more than $40,000 or so for a 9 × 12 foot room. Something a little simpler on the walls or floors will average around $50 to $75 a square foot. A nice marble tub—something you can step down into—should cost around $5000. A supersized solid marble tub could easily run $25,000. Instead of a commode, you'll want a carved wood Louis XV chamber pot. Around $700, although you can marble *it*, too, for around $2000. A gold sink—24-karat gold over porcelain—will run $250, less the fittings (an additional $300 if you want them in gold). Add around $1200 for sauna, and $150 for a bidet ($1000 if you want a marble cover for it). None of these prices, of course, includes labor. The world's best-known luxury bathroom outfitters is Sherle Wagner, whose headquarters are in New York. They also do modest bathrooms.

Sherle Wagner International, Inc.
60 East 57th St.
New York, N.Y. 10022

A HOME ELEVATOR

Something automatic that will go up two stories and hold two people: on the average, between $7500 and $10,000. Builders and installers of commercial elevators will do it. Something with a plexiglass casing so you can see the innards of your house as you go up and down will probably run you around $14,000. Muzak is extra.

A HOME SAUNA

Most of the saunas on the market today are pre-fab jobs you put together yourself. You can get them as small as 3 × 4 feet or as big as 10 × 12. They come complete with heater, controls, rocks, internal prewiring, thermometer, interior light, benches, and duct board. They are not hard to install. The smaller units run around $900 in most places. A 6 × 6 foot model will run you around $2500. The big saunas run close to $5000. Check the *Yellow Pages*.

A JACUZZI WHIRLPOOL BATHTUB

One that has the whirlpool inlets built right in. For the regular, not so fancy ones, anywhere from $900 to $1200. For the spiffy looking marbelescent ones, between $2300 and $2900. For one 55 square feet, which can accommodate as many as eight people, about $2900. Figure an additional $250 if you want the parts gold-plated, and an additional $250 if you want custom colors. Other features available. Check with a local Jacuzzi dealer.

CONVERTING YOUR SHOWER INTO A STEAM ROOM

The units themselves, which are the size of a tall attaché case, run about $450 for an area of 80 cubic feet to around $2200 for a room capable of holding about 30 people. Your shower or bath enclosure has to be completely sealed on all sides, and the bathtub walls and ceilings have to be covered with tile, Formica, or metal.

A SKYLIGHT

Unless you have a flat roof or a cathedral ceiling (most houses, alas, have pitched roofs and flat ceilings), getting a skylight put in is going to involve the building of an appropriate ceiling, a major construction job in and of itself. Assuming you have the appropriate ceiling, figure between $170 and $200 if you want to buy the skylight and install it yourself. This will buy the standard three-foot-square skylight. If you want extra insulation—a double dome model, figure around $300. Getting a contractor or builder to buy and install a skylight for you should run around $450, barring any unusual complications. That's for the square skylight. The round skylights are trickier to install and usually cost around a third more to put in.

A HOME GREENHOUSE

Home greenhouses come in a crazy mix of sizes and are priced accordingly. Window greenhouses run anywhere from $140 to $275. A 4 × 8 foot greenhouse should cost around $1000 to buy and about $80 a year to run. A major league greenhouse—1100 square feet—can run as much as $15,000 to buy and $500 a year to run. You could grow your own jungle in it. Things you need in a greenhouse include a ventilating or exhaust system, a heater, a humidifier, a cooling system, and some means of watering. Accessories run between $500 and $2000. The most economical kind of greenhouse to buy is the kind that leans against the side of your house.

SOUNDPROOFING YOUR APARTMENT (OR WHATEVER)

Your first step is to get hold of an acoustical engineer. He will charge you anywhere from $30 to $50 an hour for a written recommendation. He will tell you that you don't sound*proof* anything, you sound-*reduce* it. He will also tell you that the fact that your neighbor's toilet sounds like Niagara Falls when it flushes is not necessarily an indication that your building contractor used tissue paper to separate the apartments. Even the most expensive and solidly built buildings can cause sound problems if the acoustical engineering hasn't been well thought out.

The soundproofing itself: depending on the nature of the problem and what it takes to remedy it, the price of sound-reducing an average room (12 × 15 feet) is anywhere from $500 to $4000. The $500 usually involves the construction of a soundboard (60¢ a square foot) on the wall that separates you and your rock musician neighbor. More elaborate jobs may involve the construction of a double wall. A good pair of ear plugs runs about $2. You don't have to see a consultant.

A SWIMMING POOL

Let's be conservative and figure a 20 × 40 foot pool with a vinyl lining, a pleasant patio and all the hardware (pump, etc.) you need. As long as the site work isn't too overwhelming, figure around $12,000. Something with a concrete lining, with a nice design at the bottom and a professionally landscaped setting gets you into the $20,000 range. If you want an indoor pool, figure about $30,000 for a self-contained building: nothing great—just a prefab job. If you want to go the Hugh Hefner route, with an indoor pool that goes from room to room with glass walls and lots of underwater toys, figure a minimum of $150,000.

YOUR OWN TENNIS COURT

Not so fast. First, make sure you have the room. A regulation tennis court measures 36 × 78 feet, but that's not counting the extra room along the sides and behind each baseline. Ideally, you'd like 12 feet on each side and 21 feet behind the baseline, but you can skimp a little and it won't make that much difference. Another thing: make sure you know your local zoning ordinances, especially the amount of room you need between your fence and your neighbor's property line. Try, too, to build the court on a north-south axis, thereby avoiding the direct line of the sun in the morning and late afternoon.

Now then, if everything is go from here you're ready to talk price. The two biggest cost factors are (1) the amount of work needed to prepare the site for the court and (2) the type of surface you want. Site work can vary from $200 to $500 for a piece of real estate that is relatively flat and needs only minor grading to as much as $20,000 if your backyard resembles Mount Rushmore. The easiest court to get built is straight asphalt, like in a driveway. Not very esthetic. Not very easy on the feet. Figure around $9000 to $12,000, fencing not included. Clay or other crushed stone surfaces, like Har Tru, run between $8000 and $10,000, less fencing and sprinkling system, but you have to take care of them, sweeping and watering, etc. The new cushioned surfaces, which are easier on the feet and not as fast as asphalt, can run you from $4000 to $14,000 more than straight asphalt. Fencing adds an additional $1500 to $2000 to the bill. It's cheaper to build a court if you contract it yourself. It's also a lot more aggravating.

YOUR OWN INDOOR TENNIS COURT

Essentially it's a question of how you choose to cover it. Something esthetically pleasing in brick or bleached cypress that will draw the photographers from the architectural magazines will probably run you in the neighborhood of $150,000, not counting the court. Something not so esthetically pleasing—a pre-fab aluminum job, for instance, and that may not get by the local zoning board—will run around $90,000, light and heat included. The other option is to bubble it. An air-supported bubble that measures a foot shorter and a foot narrower than a regulation size tennis court and has a 29-foot ceiling starts at around $40,000, but you'll probably want to get a double-walled bubble—yes, a double bubble—which will run closer to $48,000. (You'll save the difference in fuel bills.) It should cost you between $8000 and $10,000 to get the thing put up, and around $5000 to heat it and light it and take it down at the end of the year and store it. With a little bit of luck, it should last you around 10 years.

YOUR OWN PLATFORM TENNIS COURT

It depends on whether you want to build the thing yourself—and it's trickier than it looks—or want to have a professional do it. If you want to do it yourself, you can get a complete kit from DeVoe Systems for around $8000, plus shipping. It's nice-looking, but will take you a while to put it up. The pros get anywhere from $12,000 for a basic wooden-floor model—not a good idea since they require yearly maintenance—to $20,000 for an all-aluminum model, complete with lights.

DeVoe Systems
800 Eastern Ave.
Carlstadt, N.J. 07202

YOUR OWN BOWLING ALLEY

Measure the basement first: you need at least 100 feet. The few people who've had them installed usually get two lanes—it's more official looking. For the alleys, the ball-return lanes, the pins, the automatic pin setters—everything but the lighting and the preliminary electrical work on the pin setters, figure around $35,000.

> Brunswick Corporation
> 1605 Jersey Ave.
> North Brunswick, N.J. 08902

YOUR OWN ENVIRONMENT CHAMBER

The thing is called "Environment." Just like that. The idea is to sit inside it, switch a dial or two, and create whatever "natural" environment tweaks your fancy. You can have "Baja Sun," "Jungle Steam," and "Chinook Winds." You can rig up a stereo soundtrack to it, too. A 7 × 3 foot fiberglass enclosure, "Environment" has cedar floors, teak walls, and 24-carat-gold rain spigots. Stripped (without stereo, art nouveau panels, and not installed), figure around $10,000. Check out your local bath dealer.

YOUR OWN FILM LIBRARY

The idea being, of course, to hear Sam play it again and again and again. It's not easy. As long as a film holds onto its copyright, prints available to the public remain in short supply. Once a copyright is given up, certain distributors buy the film and make prints. Prices vary generally according to the newness of the film. A W. C. Fields short will run you around $45. *A Star Is Born*, with Judy, not Barbra, will cost you around $500. Old-time serials are in abundant supply. The only serial Tom Mix ever made you can get for around $700. Gene Autry and Smiley Burnette in the *Phantom Empire* costs around $535. A *Casablanca* print of your own? Possible but difficult since the film's copyright keeps getting renewed. Now and then a print shows up and it runs around $250. Best advice: get on the mailing list of a company specializing in film distribution.

Storage Films
P.O. Box 4337, Hopi Station
Scottsdale, Ariz. 85258

A CASTLE IN SPAIN

Or Germany, Ireland, France, wherever. The price of a European castle depends on any number of things, among them the amount of land, the location and, obviously, the shape it's in. A number of castles still privately owned have neither electricity nor heating, which doesn't make for very pleasant living no matter how lovely the place is. Some sample prices: a 30-room castle, partially remodeled, on 30 acres, in the south of Spain, was selling not long ago for around $600,000. A fully refurbished castle in Ireland, on a river, was on the market for $2 million. The best way to figure is this: if it's been renovated, it's going to run you in excess of $1 million. If it hasn't been renovated, the minimum is probably around $300,000.

Previews, Inc.
65 E. 55th
New York, N.Y. 10022

YOUR OWN ISLAND

As with any piece of real estate, the price of an island depends mainly on where it is, how big it is, what it looks like, and what possibilities it holds for development. Generally speaking, the easier an island is to get to, the more it will cost, but there is a point at which inaccessibility becomes an attraction in its own right. Chances are the island you buy won't have electricity, but you should be more concerned with whether or not it has a fresh water source. Islands start at around $5000. This buys you an isolated acre or two somewhere in the Great Lakes, Wisconsin or Canada. You will not want to go there in February. If you want something beachy in the Caribbean, figure at least $100,000. A 70-acre island with a hotel on it was selling in the Grenadines not long ago for $350,000. A 640-acre island in the British Virgin Islands was on the block a while back for $8 million. Thirty acres in Tahiti will probably run you $150,000. A palm-swept 30-acre island in Fiji was selling recently for $225,000. Nobody knows for sure just how many islands throughout the world are in private hands. Rare Earth Realty, which specializes in island sales, knows of 900.

Rare Earth Realty
P.O. Box 946
Sausalito, Cal. 94965

YOUR OWN SOVEREIGN STATE

First, you have to acquire a place that carries with it sovereignty. Tricky, since there aren't that many places on the globe that some country hasn't laid its grubby claim to. The best strategy: seek out a country in need of cash and in possession of a few remote islands it doesn't care to hold. You should figure a minimum of $1 million. Even then you may be outbid. Some people have already indicated a willingness to spend $20 million for the right place. The advantages of sovereignty are obvious. You write your own laws, establish your own zoning ordinances, set your own minimum drinking age, select your own baseball commissioner, appoint yourself king. The United Nations is unlikely to recognize you unless you convince them that you'll vote the Third World line. You'll have trouble getting other places to recognize your currency and stamps. And unless you have an army, you're a sitting duck for any invading force.

Rare Earth Realty
P.O. Box 946
Sausalito, Cal. 94965

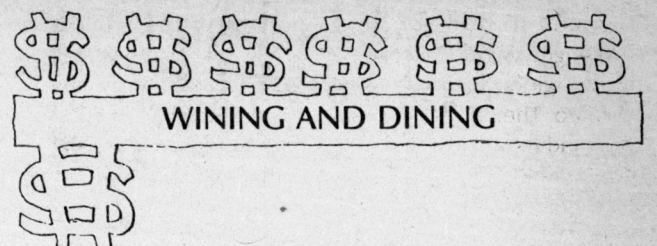

WINING AND DINING

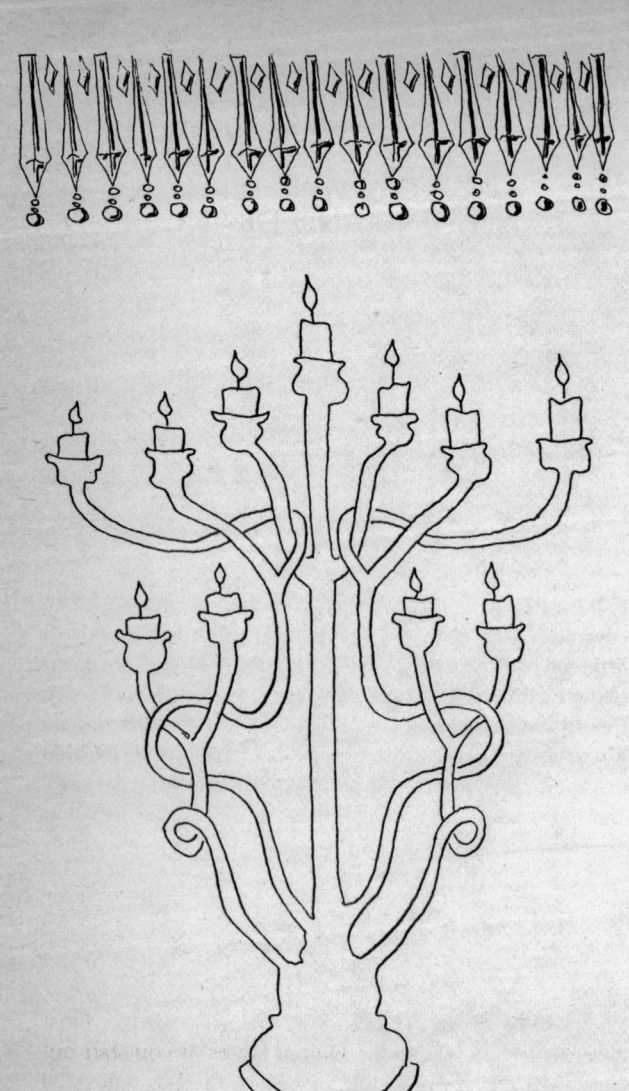

CAVIAR

The best stuff, everybody says, is the large-grain beluga caviar. You buy it in a 14-ounce can. Use it judiciously—a little on your baked potato, a dollop or two on your cottage cheese, a caviar omelet for breakfast—and a can should last about a week. Caviar can run anywhere from $70 to $140 a can, but there's no way of telling if the $140 can is all that much better than a can that costs, say, $90. The only way to find out is to eat enough so that you can differentiate. Stay with it.

DINNER AT THE PALACE

It's in New York and holds claim to being the most expensive restaurant in the United States. If you start out with a couple of pre-dinner cocktails, the tab reads $20 before you sit down to dinner. Dinner is an eight-course affair. It includes a caviar appetizer, a soup (mussels with saffron, perhaps), a fish course, a taste of lemon ice to cleanse the palate, a main course (a nice rack of veal), salad, fruits, cheeses, and desserts. The price is $60 per person.

You'll want wine. For the fish course, a 1972 Château de Meursault Comte de Maucheron: around $45. For the main course, a 1962 Château La Mission Haut Brion: $60. An after-dinner cordial will add $6 for each to the tab. It comes to around $257, but you have to figure in 8% for tax and 23% for tips. A safe figure for a dinner for two at the Palace is $328, but if you're careful about what you drink, you can probably get by for around $100 a head.

A BORDEAUX WINE TASTING

You won't do much better than 1961. Here's what you'll need: Château Lafite-Rothschild ($99.50); Château Latour ($79.50); Château Haut Brion ($75); Château Margaux ($79.50); Château Mouton-Rothschild ($99.50); Château Ansone ($75). There isn't a wine fancier in the world who would turn down your invitation.

THE OLDEST VINTAGE WINE IN THE WORLD

As far as anybody can tell, it's an 1806 Château Lafite-Rothschild, a Bordeaux that most wine authorities insist is now undrinkable. At an auction in New Orleans, in the spring of 1976, a Los Angeles oilman named David I. Lyons bought the bottle for $1,420. This price exceeded by nearly three times the previous record price paid: $500 for an 1846 Lafite.

VINTAGE LAFITE-ROTHSCHILD BY THE CASE

For a good year, like 1966, from $495 to $540. For a great year, like 1961, from $850 to $960.

DOM PERIGNON BY THE CASE

A fifth runs around $31 or so. A magnum is twice that. There are twelve in a case. You can do the multiplying.

DANDY BRANDY

You're reasonably safe with Hennessy Extra. A fifth sells for around $90. The Baccarat decanter runs $5 more.

FOIE GRAS

The only way to eat it is fresh, and the only time you can get it fresh is in November and December, which is when the French produce and export limited quantities of it. You can buy the canned foie gras year round, with the best of the lot going for about $30 for a 7-ounce can. Fresh foie gras, when you can get it, sells for around $65 a pound. Don't freeze it. Thawing breaks down its texture. If you wrap it carefully—very carefully—it can last a month in the refrigerator.

A PICNIC BASKET FROM FORTNUM & MASON

They don't call it a picnic basket in London's most famous grocery store. They call it a Luxury Hamper. In it you get champagne, malt whiskey, beluga caviar, *foie gras aux truffes,* handmade chocolates, Stilton cheese, *canard aux pruneaux,* turkey leg in a special sauce, tropical fruit cake, turtle soup, along with vintage marmalade, a fine blend of tea, and petits four. The malt whiskey comes in a hand-cut crystal decanter. Four should be able to nibble very nicely. Around $600.

A SMITHFIELD HAM

Indisputably the ham of hams. It's produced in the small Virginia town of Smithfield, where it is aged and dried in a manner unique to this area. In smaller quantities, Smithfield ham will run you between $3.50 and $4 a pound. A 13-pound ham whole will run you around $36 uncooked and $40 cooked.

A MAIL ORDER CLAMBAKE

A small but dependable number of New England food houses will put together for you just about everything you need to hold your own clambake and will mail commercial air freight. The stuff usually comes refrigerated in a special bake can. A typical serving might include a small lobster, some steamer clams, a fish fillet, vegetables and, possibly, sausage links. Depending on the size of the lobster, the price is generally between $6

and $8 per serving plus a freight charge on the can—
generally around $5. A single can can generally hold as
many as 10 servings.

Wickford Shellfish Company
67 Esmond Ave.
Wickford, R.I. 02852

SMOKED SALMON

Buy the imported Irish salmon and get it by the side—
around 2½ pounds. It will stay at least for a month. It
should run you around $25 at a specialty food shop.

GETTING AROUND

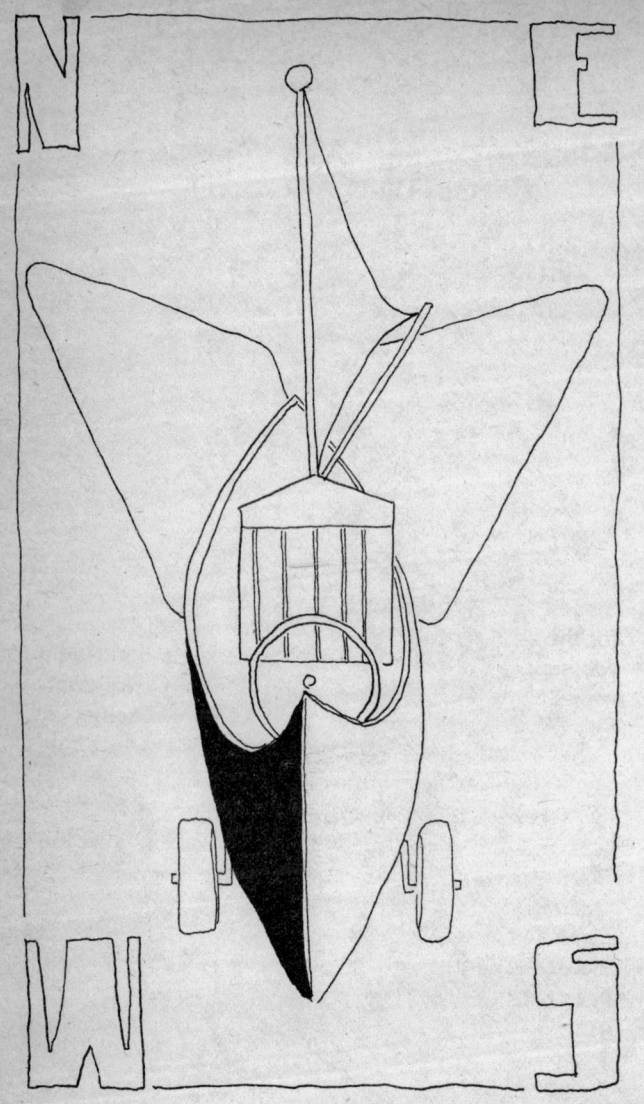

CHARTERING A PLANE

Arrange it by the mile or by the hour. Something modest—a Cherokee 6—to take you skiing or to the shore for the weekend will run anywhere from $55 an hour if you supply the pilot, about $100 an hour if the pilot comes along. Executive jets, with basic crew (two pilots) generally charter out at around $1.50 a mile, whether you arrange it by the mile or by the hour. For a DC 8—it holds 223 passengers—along with a flight crew that includes six flight attendants, a cross-country flight will run you $43,000, meals, movies, and booze included. A chartered 747 to Europe—a 747 can hold above 372 people—runs around $45,000, give or take $5000. An around-the-world flight on the same airplane, with 24 stops, will run around $300,000. If you want the Concorde, figure $16,000 an hour.

A HORSE

Buying It: for a steed that doesn't look as if it's taken too many dives in too many grade B westerns, figure a minimum of $1000. Base price for a thoroughbred is $1500. For a first-rate polo pony, figure $2500 to $4000. For a polo pony with the right blood lines, at least $7000. A backyard pony for the kids should run between $200 and $500.

Taking Care of It: horses eat like horses. Food bills for the average horse are between $2 and $3 a day. Half this is for hay. The rest is for feed. If you have to stable him at somebody else's place, the cost will depend on how much of the messy work you do for yourself. If you're not averse to handling the cleaning and the feeding, a small stable in the sticks will charge you around $50 a month. Stabling plus the rest varies from $125 to $250, depending where you live. (It's cheaper in rural areas.) If the horse is active, he'll need reshoeing every six weeks or so. Between $15 and $25. Vet fees? Add $60 to be on the safe side.

Outfitting You and Horse: it's called tack. The big-ticket item is a saddle. New, a good English saddle runs $200 and up, but you can get used saddles in reasonable shape for $100. An additional $200 should take care of the halter, the brushes, and the blanket. Try to buy the stuff from the person selling you the horse.

A CUSTOMIZED LIMOUSINE

Start with the car itself: a factory-fresh Lincoln Continental. It lists for around $13,000. You will want it stretched, which is to say lengthened to accommodate a row of seats and thus conform to accepted limousine standards.

The stretching process costs an additional $13,000. You should have an electrically operated sun roof ($1500), a power-operated window to separate you from your chauffeur ($1000), incandescent, one-way mirrored glass on the four side windows and the back so that you can see out but riffraff can't see in (around $2000). Beaver carpeting throughout will run $6000, velour upholstery another $1500. A seven-inch color television built into a console will cost $900 (you could get a bigger screen but the reception would suffer). An AM-FM quadrasonic system with a tape deck is about $1200. A phone system in which there are *two* phones: one, in the chauffeur's section (the only one that rings) and one in the back. Something with 23 channels should not cost more than $2300. A bar set up with ice storage (with drain), a crystal decanter, and a sterling silver ice bucket shouldn't cost more than $1200. So much for the basics. If you want the car bullet-proofed—that is, sheathed in a dual hardened 1¼-inch-thick steel coating capable of blunting a Magnum 44 bullet, add about $300,000 to the bill. (The White House limousine, built in 1967, cost around $500,000.) A seat in the back that can be electronically raised and lowered (a handy convenience on hunting expeditions) will run about $12,000. (Remember to open the roof before you raise the seat.) Figure six weeks for most customizing work, except for the bullet-proofing. Figure nine months if you want the car armorized. A $4000 deposit (apart from the price of the car) will be required on normal customizing work. For the armor job, you'll have to pay a third in the beginning, a third more after six months, and the final third three weeks before the car is delivered.

Moloney Coach Builders
5300 Newport Ave.
Rolling Meadow, Ill. 60008

YOUR OWN PLANE

The plane itself: for a single-engine two-seater—something to tool around in on a Sunday afternoon—figure $12,000 to $15,000 used, and $20,000 new. For a six-seater, something that will cruise at about 200 to 220 mph, figure on at least $35,000, and about $22,000 used. The class of the single-engine field, the Beechcraft Bonanza, retails for $75,000 new and $30,000 used. For something in a two-engine model, count on spending $150,000. A very modest executive jet, the Cessna Citation, costs $800,000.

Running it: the smaller the plane, the less you'll spend. Insurance on a plane worth $15,000 is about $500 a year. Tie-down fees at an airport run anywhere from $10 a month in the sticks to $75 a month in a big city airport. Annual inspection and regular maintenance: about $300. Gas? If you fly 100 hours, figure $7.50 an hour, or $750. Your radio will need yearly servicing: another $200. An engine overhaul, when it becomes necessary, is $3000 to $5000. All told, excluding overhaul and purchase price, owning a small plane should run you between $3500 and $5000 a year.

YOUR OWN HELICOPTER

Something to whisk you from home to your midtown office in minutes, spare you the misery of weekend traffic jams. The 206B JetRanger, made by Bell Helicopter, in Fort Worth, will serve nicely. It seats four, plus the pilot, can travel at around 130 mph, and has a range of 350 miles. The luggage compartment holds five two-suiters. Base price is $185,000 new. Pop out floats, in case, God forbid, you have to land in water, cost an additional $28,000. An extra $5000 buys the fancy interior. The heater costs $5000. For operating cost, figure about $50 an hour, not counting the pilot, whom you'll have to pay upwards of $20,000 per year. Insurance is another $9000. Depreciation over seven years is about $18,500.

A HELI-HOME

Take one S-58 Sikorsky helicopter and combine it with a Winnebago motor home and what do you get? A flying recreational vehicle. The typical Heli-Home accommodates about eight passengers on Pullman seats (not counting the pilot in the cockpit). It is air conditioned, has a toilet and shower, a refrigerator, electric stove, and color TV. It will travel around 100 mph and will, of course, land in a lot of places inaccessible to standard aircraft. Figure around $300,000 if you want to buy one. Figure $10,000 a week, plus the pilot, if you want to rent one. Check with your local Winnebago dealer.

BUYING A MERCEDES-BENZ IN GERMANY AND SHIPPING IT BACK

Let's take the 450SLC Coupe Automatic. Stripped, it's going to run you in the States around $27,000, plus taxes. Pick it up at the factory in Stuttgart—they'll throw in a tour of the place free, and you'll spend about $4500 less. Now you have to get it back. Shipping is about $600. Marine insurance about $400. Duty (depending on the mileage) around $575. Land insurance in Europe around $625. The bottom line: you save around $2000, which incidentally is about what it would cost you for a 10-day European vacation.

AN ELECTRIC CAR

The good news is that you can throw away your gas credit card. The bad news is that you can only go between 30 and 45 miles on one charge. One American company, Sebrin-Vanguard, Inc., is mass-producing electric cars, its line consisting of two models: one with a limit of 28 mph, at $2500, and one with a limit of 38 mph, at $3800. An Ohio company, Electric Vehicle Associates, Inc., is importing a model that can hit 55 mph, but it costs $7000, not including utilities.

A SPORTIER CAR

A Ferrari, say. Figure around $25,000 for the economy model—the 308 GT4 and $54,000 for the 365 GT4, which can travel around 200 miles an hour and offers a ride that is described by one of its owners as "sex in motion." Ferrari also has a prototype car—the Pininfarina—that supposedly combines the latest in aerodynamic styling (even the door handles are electronic so as not to be a source of drag) with a number of safety features. You can probably get it for $150,000. Porsches: Figure around $11,500 if you want the 924 well equipped; $17,000 for the most popular model, the 911; and around $30,000 for the new Turbo model, which has an electronic sliding glass roof. Triumphs: anywhere between $5500 and $7000, with the midget Spitfire going for around $4500. The Lotus Esprit will run you around $19,500. Alfa Romeos: around $9000. Maseratis: either $25,000 or $38,000 depending on the size of the engine. Lamborghini—possibly the fastest production car in the world, if you buy the Countach model: around $52,000.

A CUSTOM CAR

A bed? A soup can? A stagecoach? The Batmobile? You can customize a car to resemble almost anything in the world, providing you go to the right place. And the right place for the movie and television industry is Barris Industries, Inc., in North Hollywood, which designs and builds the super special road jobs seen in the movies and on television. Barris designed and built the Batmobile for $85,000. A car done up to look like a Campbell's Soup can costs around $22,000. The 1849 stagecoach with two engines built for the rock group Paul Revere costs $80,000. Complete customizing jobs can run anywhere from $30,000 to $100,000. A more pedestrian job—like putting a T-top on your Cadillac—will run around $1200.

Barris Industries, Inc.
10811 Riverside Drive
North Hollywood, Cal. 91602

A SAILBOAT

Size and features are the two chief variables that color the sailboat price spectrum. At the bottom end, you have the Sunfish—simple to sail and holding two people. A big toy. New, around $750 (cheaper in discount stores). Used, from $350 to $500. For the reasonably serious sailing novitiate, a 13- or 14-foot Blue Jay (Blue Jay is a classification, not a trade name) should suffice. New, around $2000. Used, between $1000 and $1200. Next step up in class is the Lightning, a bigger version of the Blue Jay. Around 20 feet. New, about $4000. Used, $2500. After the Lightning comes not the Thunder but the Ensign. It sleeps two, and you can put a head (toilet) in it. New,

$6000. Used, $3500 to $4000. Once you get past the Ensign stage, it's a matter of what you want to do with it: race or just cruise around. A 27-foot cruising boat with a galley, a head, a dinette that seats four and converts to a berth, and sleeping accommodations runs around $20,000 new and $10,000 used. Less elaborate 27-footers start at around $13,000. A 33-foot racing boat could easily cost $65,000.

A YACHT

"Yacht" is a subjective term you can use to describe *anything* that moves in the water, but generally the term describes a pleasure boat—whether it's a sailing vessel or a power vessel—that measures in excess of 30 feet and provides more than a modicum of creature comforts for the people on board. The price will be determined by who manufactured it, what sort of features it has, how big it is, and how old it is. The blue ribbon names in the yachting field include C & C, Pearson, Tartan, and Hinckley. A Hinckley Southwester 50-footer, new, will run around $250,000. A used Hinckley 41-foot sloop that sleeps six and is suitable for competition will probably run around $40,000. A used 47-foot Chris Craft with diesel engines and sleeping accommodations for six should run you, used, around $100,000. Something custom-built in a 66-foot yacht fisherman will run close to $700,000, used. The late Charlie Revson spent more than $3 million to buy and outfit the *Ultima II*. A Presidential yacht sold at auction (sealed bids) for around $250,000. A safe minimum for a *yacht* yacht is $20,000 for a sailing vessel, and around $25,000 for a power boat.

YOUR OWN SUBMARINE

You'll have to compromise. Buying your everyday Navy submarine with torpedos and periscopes and all is pretty much out of the question since by the time the Navy gets finished stripping them of all their electronic gear and weaponry, there's nothing too much left to fool around with. Narrow your sights. Perry Submarines, which specializes in underwater craft for the offshore industry, will fix you up with a nice two-man submarine that will travel around 5 miles an hour and take you down as far as 12,000 feet. Figure around $200,000.

> Perry Oceanographics Inc.
> 100 E. 17th St.
> Riviera Beach, Fla. 33404

A ROLLS-ROYCE

As the owners say, you're not buying a car, you're making an investment. There is no word in Rolls-Royce language for depreciation. The lineup goes like this: for the Silver Streak, around $39,000; for the Corniche Coupe, $64,000; for the Corniche Convertible, $68,000. The pride of the fleet, the Camargue, runs $96,000. No car on the market comes with more opulent features, but you can always add your own improvements. A bar in the back seat will probably cost around $2000. Figure $10,000 if you want it in teak. A hand-inlaid backgammon set should run you around $2000 (you can do it for $500, if you shop around), and if you'd like the rear seat to convert to a bed you can get it done for around $7000. Your insurance costs will depend on the model: figure around 10% of the selling price. Repairs are in the same general ballpark. A new set of shock absorbers will run around $1200. A new paint job, about $4000. A simple tune-up, around $200. Rolls owners consider themselves lucky when the service bill they receive does not exceed $500.

YOUR OWN JET

Something very basic, bare bones: a Lear Jet will run you, new, around $1.8 million. But it only seats around six and there's a limit to what you can do inside to make it more—well, *you*. Better to spend around $6 million for the Grumman Gulf Stream II. It has a range of 5000 miles and can cruise at around 600 mph. You'll want to customize it. A number of companies do this sort of work and are good about not telling anybody how much you've spent or what you've done. You're limited to some extent—FAA regulations and all—but you can still put in your own galley, stereo system and conference tables, and the FAA won't care if you outfit the head with golf fixtures. Among the things on some of the Gulf Stream II's now flying the skies are: a pipe organ, a custom-built watermelon cooler, and a built-in video system. Regardless of how hard you try, it will be hard to spend more than $1.2 million for all the interior appointments.

YOUR OWN CARGO SHIP

You pay by the ton, the age, the condition, the equipment. An average-sized cargo ship with a capacity of 35,000 tons will run you around $5 million new and about $2½ million for a ship around 10 years old. The newer ships, which are largely automated, take a crew of about 20. The older ships need around 35. Something smaller, suitable for setting up your own shipping business in the Caribbean, gets you into the 6000-ton capacity. Figure a minimum of $300,000.

AN AUGUSTA MOTORCYCLE

Completely hand assembled in Italy and one of the handful of cycles in which there is a drive shaft instead of a chain. On a straightaway, you can do 120 mph with it. When the helicopter company that produces it was limiting the number of finished models, the price was around $6,500. At last look it was $5,500.

FUN AND GAMES

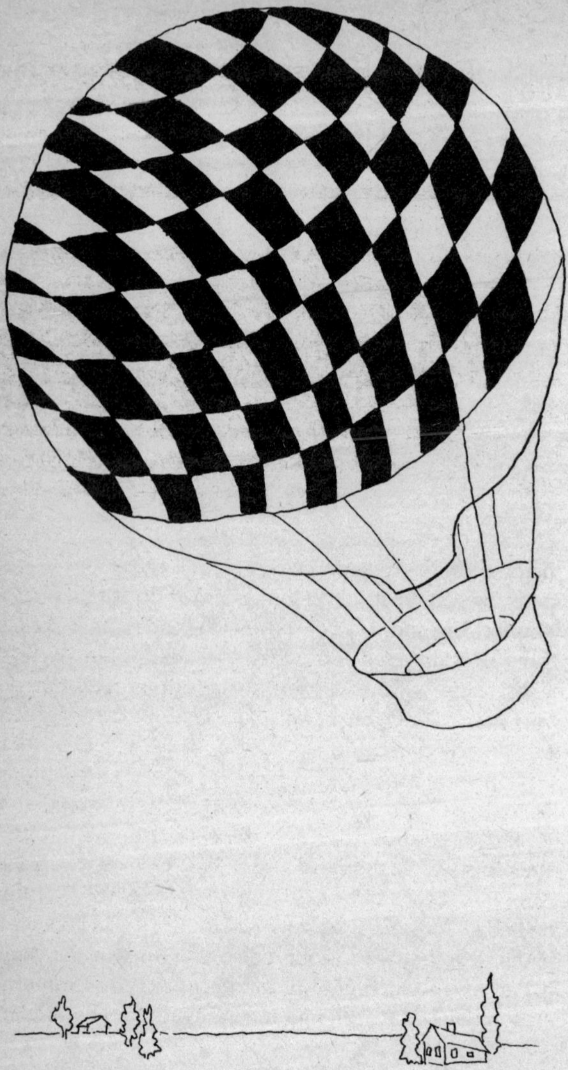

HANG GLIDING

There are safer pursuits—obviously. When you go hang gliding—or, as people often refer to it, soaring—you harness yourself to a motorless, kite-like contraption that does for you what wings and a motor do for an airplane. You fly. The sport is not as suicidal today as it was, say, three or four years ago, when the equipment wasn't as good or the instruction not as well organized but don't tell your insurance man about it. To get started, go to an established hang gliding school. Your first lesson will probably run around $35. You'll start off, if possible, in a "safe" area, like a sand dune. Within two days, if you have average athletic ability, you should be able to fly for short distances about 30 or 40 feet above the ground. After two weeks of instruction—$300 to $400—you should be ready for some advanced flying. The average hang glider sells new for around $1000. You can get a used glider in good condition for around $600. Something elaborate like a Rogallo glider (Rogallo is to hang gliding what the Wright brothers were to airplanes) will run $3000.

WHITE WATER CANOEING

The classic white water experience is canoeing down a river boiling with rapids the way Burt Reynolds and the group did it in *Deliverance*. It's also the *hardest* way to do it. Easier is the same trip via kayak (since there is more enclosed space, a kayak doesn't tip as easily). Easier still is a group trip in a large rubber raft. The generic term for the whole business is "river running," and the variations are almost endless. A one-day excursion down the relatively quiet river in the Grand Canyon might run around $30. Going down the Chattooga, where they filmed *Deliverance*, in a raft for a day costs you around $25 if you do it through the Nantahala Outdoor Center. River expeditions on rafts run anywhere from five days to two weeks. Typically, you'll travel with about eight other people in a rubber raft that ranges from 15 to 30 feet. On multi-day trips, you will stop at designated campsites along the route. The campsites are on the crude side, but well outfitted. The only things you'll have to bring along are a sleeping bag, an air mattress, personal gear, and your own booze. (Store it in plastic bottles.) Some river trip organizations expect you to bring your own tent, but most places will rent you everything you need for a few dollars a night.

Prices for each of these water adventures average from $30 to $80 a day. The difference usually has to do with creature comforts. On the more expensive trips, they usually have portable baths and showers, and the boats are a little larger and more comfortable. These prices, incidentally, do not include the cost of getting you to the river. In most places, figure your airfare, plus about $40 for the helicopter or charter plane fee.

HELICOPTER SKIING

Everybody who does it agrees that skiing would be the quintessential leisure experience if it weren't for long lift lines, other skiers, and ice patches on the slopes. Helicopter skiing spares you these inconveniences. A helicopter whisks you and a small circle of your skiing friends to a remote mountain slope unreachable via normal means. The powder there is usually so fluffy you can almost swim in it. It's tricky to ski—you should be a strong intermediate—and there is always the danger of an avalanche (although most places that offer helicopter skiing take elaborate safety measures). Helicopter skiing is relatively rare in Europe, where most of the top slopes are accessible, but you can do it on this side of the Atlantic in places like Sun Valley, Idaho; Snowbird, in Utah; Jackson Hole, in Wyoming; Mt. Hood, in California; and Bannis, in Canada. The prices vary somewhat from place to place, but usually you book by the half-day or full day, with the helicopter taking you up for anywhere from three to seven runs. At Snowbird, the price is around $115 per person for seven runs, which includes one guide for every seven skiers. On average, you'll pay around $16 a ride wherever you go.

PARACHUTE JUMPING

You could enlist in the Army or Marines and go airborne, but that's a draconian approach to a simple situation.

There are throughout the country parachute jumping organizations that will have you jumping out of an airplane less than three hours after you pay the money and sign the disclaimer. The jump is preceded by three hours of instruction. Your equipment includes *two* parachutes (an automatically deployed main chute and a reserve chute that has a radio receiver). After the jump, which is targeted to a "safe" area, you get a critique from your jump instructor ("Um ... it was fine, except it's better to pull the cord *after* you leave the plane"), a diploma, and a pin. All in all, it's as safe as these things can be. Prices for the one-day adventure start at $70, which buys you everything. Additional jumps on the same day are $13.50. Insurance is available.

POLO

The assumption is you already know how to ride a horse—well enough to play without killing yourself. Your main concern, naturally, are your ponies. For serious polo, you'll need at least five, preferably six. For casual polo, three will suffice. A good polo pony will run you between $2500 and $4000. Something the Maharajah of Jaipur might have ridden will run $8000. Figure $1000 a year to feed each horse, an additional $1000 for shoeing and vet fees. If you don't have your own stables, figure between $100 and $150 per pony a month for stabling fees (that's counting feed). Your basic equipment—helmet, breeches, shirts, knee guards, boots, breastplate, etc.—shouldn't run you more than $300. Figure another $200 for the saddle. You'll need a van (you can rent one but, in the long run, it's better to own it): $14,000 buys you a standard horse van, or you can buy a pick up truck ($5000) and a van extension ($7500). Polo club memberships run between $400 and $1500 a year. All told, you can figure an additional investment of between $35,000 and $40,000 to get you into the big leagues. From thereon in, it should cost around $15,000 a year—less if you intend to play in the west, more if you intend to play in Argentina.

SCUBA DIVING

For the basics, you'll need a serviceable troika of snorkel, mask, and fins. Figure $30. You can go as high as $70. That will do for you roughly the same what a hollowed-out reed did for Tarzan. To make the transition from snorkeling to scuba diving, figure the following: (1) air tank and valve, $100 ($140 or more for the newer and larger tanks); (2) a back pack to hold the cylinder, about $20; (3) a buoyancy vest (very important), from $60 to $220; (4) a regulator to control air pressure, from $75; and (5) a depth gauge to tell how far down you are, from $7 (down to 40 feet) to $60.

Keep your checkbook out. If you want to do cold water diving—colder than 60 degrees—you will want a custom-fitted wet suit, $150. The sartorial ultimate in a dry suit costs around $400. Underwater watches are about $75. None of which is to mention underwater toolery: a knife to extricate you from difficulties, from $15; a spear gun, from $25 to $100; a (heaven help you) shark dart, about $60. A serviceable underwater flashlight is about $15 (less batteries). Figure another $50 for accessories.

All told, you can outfit yourself for diving quite royally for around $700, but if you're looking to keep pace with the professionals, figure easily four times that figure.

CROSS-COUNTRY SKIING

Hurry, before it gets too complicated and organized. The basics—skis, bindings, boots, and poles—you can get for $100, but there are different types of skis. The most popular are the light touring skis, heavier and sturdier than racing skis but not as heavy as the touring or the mountaineering skis.

HOT-AIR BALLOONING

Mostly it's a matter of how big a balloon or, to be more specific, how big an envelope, the envelope being the whatsit that gets filled with hot air and takes you up into the wild blue yonder. Envelope sizes range from 33,000 to 105,000 cubic feet of air capacity. The smaller jobs can hold more than two people. The larger ones can carry four, counting the pilot. The price range is $3000 to $10,000. Private hot-air ballooning lessons run in the neighborhood of $125 to $175 an hour. The Balloon Ranch, in Del Norte, Colorado, has a five-day package that runs $130 per person, including your food, lodging, and group lessons.

AUTOGRAPH COLLECTING

No snickers, please. There is more to autograph collecting (or, as the world's foremost autograph dealer Charles Hamilton likes to call it, "philography") than hounding celebrities for their John Henries. Collectors in this field are drawn mainly to documents and letters, with price depending not only on whose signature graces the document but what the thing says and what its historical significance happens to be. A simple signature of Abe Lincoln is probably worth around $250 on today's market. Altman's has a line of signed photographs, matted and framed, of people like Tallulah Bankhead ($85), Boris Karloff ($85), and Ellen Terry ($65). The most expensive document sold at auction in recent years was a letter from George Washington, but the Horchow Collection not long ago was offering, for $67,500, the letter that Lincoln wrote to Grace Bedell in which he announced his intention to grow a beard. Letters from Jimmy Carter are now selling for $900, but only if they go beyond the normal form letter shtick. Letters from William Faulkner, James Joyce, Ernest Hemingway, and T. S. Eliot sell in the $1000 to $1500 range, regardless of what they say. An Emily Dickinson letter, signed "Emily" in pencil, was offered by the Horchow Collection for $4150. And a two-page original music manuscript by Mozart has been valued at $15,000.

Horchow Collection
P.O. Box 34257
Dallas, Tex. 75234

FALCONRY

Very big in the oil sheikhdoms. What it is, is hunting with a falcon instead of a gun. Then again, you have to spend a lot of time training the falcon, which means spending a lot of time with the bird on your heavily gloved fist for several hours a day while you talk to it, stroke it and, in general, get it to relax. There are less than 3000 registered falconers in the world. One of them is Sheikh Zayed bin Sultan, a sportsman from Abu Dhabi, who owns 140 peregrine falcons. The peregrine is the one you want. For a good one, figure between $7000 and $10,000.

LEISURE HIGHS

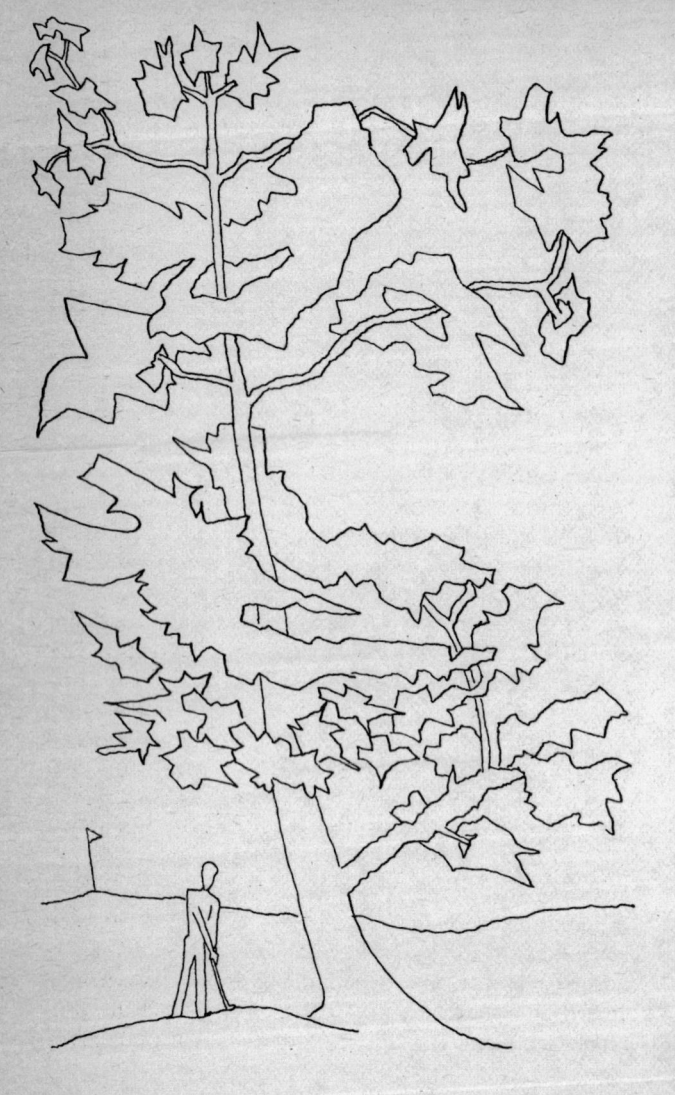

A GREAT WHITE SHARK EXPEDITION

Great white sharks frolic in the chilly waters off South Australia, and See & Sea Travel Service, in San Francisco, will take you there for a personal look-see providing you are an experienced diver with legitimate photographic objectives. Your group will be led by Rodney Fox, possibly the world's best authority on sharks. For company you'll have Ron and Valerie Taylor, two Australian superstars of underwater film-making. The way it works is that your group goes out in a two boat tandem. One boat baits the sharks. When they arrive, you slip into one of the shark cages moored along the side of the boat. The shark cages go down and you get a chance to experience firsthand what it's like to be almost nose to nose with a 16-foot maneater. The really exciting part, though, is when one of the sharks "nudges" your cage when you're not expecting it. The expedition lasts 14 days. You're cruising for sharks for seven days, going back to your hotel each night. The rest of the time is spent in Sydney or en route. The first great white shark expedition, in 1976, was a big success, but the expedition stirred up a lot of rancor in Australia—reports began to spread that the expedition was *luring* sharks to the populated areas—and had to be postponed in 1977. At last word, See & Sea was setting something up for 1978. The price is $4000 a person, not including airfare: around $1350 from the West Coast and $1700 from New York.

See & Sea Travel Service, Inc.
680 Beach St., Suite 340
Wharfside
San Francisco, Cal. 94109

A RED BARON AIRPLANE RIDE

All you need is the right plane, goggles, a strong stomach, and a fertile imagination. A number of specialty air services around the country, among them Simsbury Air Service in Simsbury, Conn., will supply the plane and the goggles. You supply the strong stomach and the imagination. At Simsbury, your plane is a Stearman PT 13, an early World War II bi-wing trainer with an open cockpit and a handcranked wooden propeller. The pilot will take you through a series of loops, spins, and rolls. You simulate the machinegun fire. The price for 15 minutes of simulated air combat is $20; $60 buys you an hour. There is no insurance for combat fatigue.

Simsbury Air Service
Simsbury Airport
Simsbury, Conn. 06070

A GAME OF ONE ON ONE WITH DR. J.

You set the ground rules. You can allow flying slammer dunks but prohibit reverse twists. Or any variations thereof. Dr. J. (and if you don't know that Dr. J. is Julius Erving of the Philadelphia 76ers you don't deserve to play one on one with him) will, under certain conditions, show up at your driveway basketball hoop for a short session, but he's reluctant to talk price and you'll probably have to deal with his agent, Irwin Weiner. A lot of it will depend on why you're doing it. If it's a charity that the doctor believes in or if you're a friend of a friend of a friend, you may get him for a lot less than you might imagine. Otherwise, the bidding will probably start around the $7500 mark, and nobody will give any promises one way or the other.

Walt Frazier Enterprises
370 Lexington Ave.
New York, N.Y. 10017

AN EXPEDITION TO THE TOP OF MOUNT EVEREST

The 11-person team that climbed the 29,082-foot mountain in 1976 used 200 oxygen bottles, camping gear, and food for 47 people (there were six cameramen and 30 sherpas). The expedition took two months. The estimated budget of $200,000 fell $90,000 short.

A GRIZZLY BEAR HUNT IN THE YUKON

The fact is, you don't hunt a grizzly bear (bears never hang out in one particular place): you simply run into one, if you're lucky. Or unlucky. In any case you make arrangements ahead of time with a Yukon outfitter (i.e., guide), who will meet you at the airport in White Horse. (You fly in from Edmonton or Montreal, etc.) You stay a night in a hotel in White Horse and next morning fly out to a base camp that's generally next to a well-stocked lake. You sleep in a tent on a cot. You eat like a sultan. After two days at the base camp, you and the rest of the hunters in the party ride horses into the so-called spike camp, and it's from here that you do your heavy hunting. Most hunts involve not only grizzlies but moose, caribou, and Dall sheep. You get trophies of whatever you shoot. Hunts of this nature seem particularly popular among high-pressure executives some of whom come here for post heart attack R&R. Some outfitters will permit no booze, so check that out ahead of time. Most outfitters go out of their way to be accommodating, and they keep the camps well-maintained or else risk losing their licenses. The Yukon hunting season isn't too long. It starts August 1 and is over by September 30. The weather is agreeable at this time of year—rarely hotter than 80 during the day and quite cool at night. Typical costs for a Yukon adventure are $300 a day, everything included but your guns, ammo, and sleeping, for which you are responsible. Read the outdoor magazines for leads.

ROD LAVER AS YOUR DOUBLES PARTNER

Or Ilie Nastase, Bjorn Borg, Arthur Ashe, et al. If they have the time and you provide first class air accommodations and all incidental expenses plus the fee, you can usually hire a superstar tennis player for between $7500 and $10,000 a day. You have to make arrangements through their agents. The players make the final decision.

Dell, Craighill, Fentress & Benton
1200 Brawner Bldg.
888 17th St. N.W.
Washington, D.C. 20006

International Management
2 Erie View Plaza
Cleveland, Ohio 44114

A ROUND OF GOLF AT THE AUGUSTA NATIONAL

Cypress Point, at Pebble Beach, California, may be a more spectacular looking golf course, but the Augusta National Golf Club, in Augusta, Georgia, comes as close to the ultimate golfing experience as any golfer has a right to expect. The 7000-yard par 72 course came into being because of Bobby Jones and is the site each year of the Masters Tournament. The fairways are wide and there is no rough, but the greens are large and difficult to read. Mostly, though, what makes the Augusta so special is the pastoral setting. The place was built on what used to be a nursery, and no course in the world is more impeccably maintained or more gloriously flowered. The highlight for most golfers is the 13th hole, with its 8000 azalea plants.

To play here, you have to be a guest of a member. The green fees are $25, and the caddy will run you around $15. The clubhouse food is not up to the course but the wine list is impressive.

A SKIING WEEKEND WITH JEAN CLAUDE KILLY

With the understanding, of course, that the triple gold medal winner in the 1968 Olympics will give you some personal instruction and hang out a little with you at dinner, etc. Schedule permitting, Killy's weekend fee is $10,000, plus all expenses.

International Management
2 Erie View Plaza
Cleveland, Ohio 44114

A MOTORCYCLE RIDE WITH EVEL KNIEVEL

For his barrel-jumping derring-do at state fairs and the like, Evel gets anywhere from $25,000 to $50,000. A ride with Evel—you on your bike and he on his—is possible, but with lots of conditions. He has to have the time, has to be in the mood, and isn't about to risk his neck on your ego trip. If all systems are go, you can figure a minimum of $12,000 for an hour's ride.

International Creative Management
40 W. 57th St.
New York, N.Y. 10022

DIVING FOR SPANISH GOLD

You dive for Spanish gold at the bottom of Tobermory Bay, in Scotland. A licensed diver sets it all up and supplies all the gear. You stay at the Duke of Argyll's castle, in Inverary. Sakowitz offers it for $50,000 for two people—good for a weekend's divertissement.

> Sakowitz
> 1111 Main St.
> Houston, Tex. 77002

A ROUND IN THE RING WITH MUHAMMAD ALI

He'll float like a butterfly and sting like a bee,
As long as you're willing to pay his exhibition fee.
$100,000.

> Don King Enterprises
> 30 Rockefeller Center
> New York, N.Y. 10020

DICK SQUIRES AS YOUR PADDLE PARTNER

If you don't know who Dick Squires is, you don't deserve to be playing platform tennis (also known as paddle). Until a few years ago, Squires was the perennial champion in the sport. He is the author of two books. His daily fee is $500.

> Dick Squires
> 7 Pond St.
> Rowayton, Conn. 06883

TOBOGGANING DOWN THE CRESTA
BLANCA TOBOGGAN RUN

The fabled sled run at St. Moritz, in the Swiss Alps, runs about three-quarters of a mile, with a drop of about 514 feet. Hairy! With the toe rakes you wear and with strong enough legs, you can pretty much crawl down—the way Errol Flynn did the only time he ventured down the hazardous run—but nobody in the Kulm Hotel will want to have anything to do with you later. Then again, if you go *too* fast—especially around the Shuttlecock Curve—nobody in the Kulm Hotel will be *able* to have anything to do with you later. Most of the sledders who challenge the run belong to the ultra exclusive St. Moritz Toboggan Club, more a social club than a tobogganing club. If you're just passing through, you can ride the Cresta from the Junction starting point down to a point a quarter of the way short of the entire run. The cost is around $40, and the tobogganing season runs from late December to late February. Women are not—repeat, not—allowed to make the run.

SKIING AT ZURS

Zurs is one of four villages—the other three are St. Anton, St. Christoph, and Lech—that help explain why most ski mavens consider the Arlberg area of the Austrian Alps the world's most appealing ski paradise. There is abundant snow; the winter weather is mild and sunny; the lifts are a short walk from your hotel and there are marvelously atmospheric inns. Zurs is the smallest of the four, but its slopes are such that you can take advantage of both the early morning and late afternoon sun and it tends to be a little more jet-setty. The place to stay is the Hotel

Zeurshof. It will cost you around $500 for the week for two people. Lift tickets will run you around $65 for the week. A day of private instruction goes for around $50. If you stay in Zurs, you can ski at St. Anton, St. Christoph, and Lech thanks to crisscrossing lifts, trains, and minibuses.

A TOUR THAT FOLLOWS JOAN OF ARC'S FOOTSTEPS

You start out in the Meuse valley, visiting the peasant house where Joan was born. From there it's to all the places that figured in Joan of Arc's life—from Bourges to Chinon to Orleans and, finally, to Rouen. Around $1500 for a 16-day tour, not counting air fare.

Lindblad Travel
133 E. 55th St.
New York, N.Y. 10022

THE ALPS BY MULE

It beats walking, but not by much. The week-long mule trip takes you through the Valais section of the Alps, near the French and Italian borders. About $170 takes care of the mule, the inn accommodations, and the food. Air fare is extra.

Swiss National Tourist Board
608 Fifth Ave.
New York, N.Y. 10020

A RIDE WITH JACKIE STEWART THROUGH THE GRAND PRIX RUN AT MONACO

You provide the Porsche or Ferrari or whatever, and Jackie Stewart will show you firsthand what it feels like to peel rubber along the Grand Prix run at Monaco. There are a lot of "ifs" (if he's in the area and available, etc.), but assuming you can work out the logistics, the price for the ride should be around $5000.

International Management
2 Erie View Plaza
Cleveland, Ohio 44114

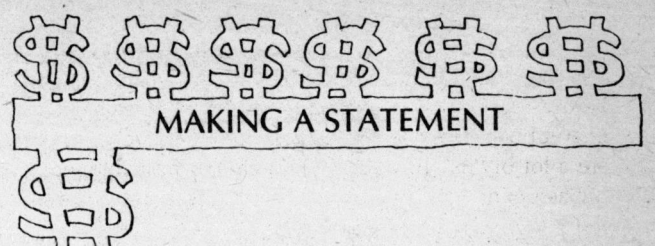

MAKING A STATEMENT

A FULL-PAGE AD IN A BIG NEWSPAPER

Newspaper rates for full-page ads vary according to any number of criteria, among them the type of product you're advertising, the day of the week the ad is running, and the frequency of the ad. Generally speaking, a full-page ad in the daily *New York Times* is going to run you around $13,000—more for Sunday and less if it's a political ad. The *Daily News* in New York gets anywhere from $8600 to $11,000. The *Washington Post* comes in at around $11,000 for the average ad. And the *National Enquirer*, with its 4 million circulation, charges around $12,000.

A CLASSIFIED AD ON THE FRONT PAGE OF THE NEW YORK TIMES

From Monday to Saturday, $42 a line and you have to buy a minimum of two lines. On Sunday, $54. Each line has 50 characters.

A CELEBRITY TO HUCKSTER YOUR PRODUCT

The money you have to surrender to a well-known entertainer, athlete, or public figure to go on the tube and tell everyone how super your product is will vary not only according to the stature of the person but according to his previous identification with commercials. A number of celebrities, for now at least, will not do a commercial for any price (Barbra Streisand, Paul Newman, Robert Redford, Gerald Ford), but their ranks keep getting slimmer and slimmer. Starting price for a well recognized name is around $50,000. That's what Jimmy Connors got for the Canada Dry spot, what Eddie Arnold got for talking about pancake syrup, and what Phyllis George would want if you wanted her. If you want Muhammad Ali, you'll have to spend at least $100,000 for a local spot but $150,000 to $200,000 for a national campaign. Word is that Gregory Peck received $250,000 to talk about Travellers Insurance, which is roughly what Chanel pays to Catherine Deneuve. James Coburn reportedly got $500,000 for appearing in a Schlitz Light commercial in which he said only two words: "Schlitz Light." Rex Harrison is said to have received $300,000 to peddle Dodges, and John Wayne supposedly got $400,000 to sit on a horse and talk about Datril—it took him about two hours. Steve McQueen received something like $1 million to endorse Honda motorcycles in Japan.

PUBLISHING YOUR OWN BOOK

What do the typical book publishers know about great writing? Obviously zilch. Why else would all be blind to the brilliance of a manuscript that everyone you know considers maybe a notch or two beneath Joyce and Dostoyevsky. Help is at hand. There are several companies—two major ones—who engage in what is known as vanity or subsidy publishing. Once they accept the manuscript—and there are occasional rejections—they'll edit the manuscript, design the book, print it, distribute it, and advertise it. You pay a substantial percentage of the freight, but you get a 40% share of the retail sales—four times what you'd get in a standard publishing deal. The whole process takes about two months and, if nothing else, you'll have Christmas presents for everybody on your list. Costs vary according to how many pages in the book, what sort of design problems you get into, and how many copies you want printed. Exposition Press will publish 750 copies of a 64-page book, between 12,000 and 15,000 words, for about $1600. They'll probably sell it for $4.50 or $5. An average novel, 60,000 words or so, would run you around $6500 for a run of 3500 copies. Start getting into the *War and Peace* league and you're talking upwards of $10,000.

Exposition Press
900 S. Oyster Bay Rd.
Hicksville, N.Y. 11801

Vantage Press
516 W. 34th St.
New York, N.Y. 10001

YOUR MESSAGE FLASHED IN LIGHTS ON TIMES SQUARE

The ribbon of lights that trumpets messages from the building at the corner of Seventh Avenue (it used to be called the Allied Chemical Building) can be your pulpit for anywhere from 30 seconds up to an hour each night between midnight and 1 A.M. The base price is 10 words for $25, with the message playing once for 30 seconds. Repeats run $15.

Spectacolor
1 Times Square
New York, N.Y. 10036

LIGHTING UP THE EIFFEL TOWER

From October 15 until the start of the tourist season in late May, the Eiffel Tower remains unlit. Not quite. If you contact the Service de l'Eclairage Publique in City Hall 48 hours in advance, you can arrange to have the Tower lit at a predetermined time, for an hour. Why would you do such a thing? For starters, as a grand gesture to a new (or old) love. The cost is $85. The same deal applies to the Arc de Triomphe for $50.

COMMERCIAL TIME ON TELEVISION

In early 1977, the major networks were getting between $50,000 and $80,000 for prime time 30-second spots—the higher fees going for the more popular shows, as determined by the ratings. Otherwise, it's a very negotiable situation. Generally, commercial time on television varies according to *when* you're buying and how many spots are involved. A network news spot within the last couple of years has been running between $16,000 and $18,000. Something sandwiched in between sermonette and the

160

National Anthem might cost you $2500 or less on some stations. The more spots you buy, the cheaper the unit price.

A BIG-TIME MADISON AVENUE ADVERTISING AGENCY TO HANDLE YOUR ACCOUNT

Unless you're going to spend in the neighborhood of $1 million a year on advertising, the top dogs on Madison Avenue—Ogilvy, Doyle Dane, J. Walter Thompson, Benton and Bowles, etc.—will not show much interest in you, unless you can demonstrate to them somehow that your company is about to make a big move. Some companies set a minimum of $3 million.

REST AND RECREATION

A WEEK AT A CHÂTEAU IN BRITTANY

About 260 miles northwest of Paris, in the province of Brittany, sits the Gothic-flavored village of Rochefort-en-Terre, and on the outskirts of the village is a privately owned château whose salons and suites are a mini-museum of priceless antiques and paintings. From June to mid-September you can stay here in your choice of accommodations: a first-floor suite with a huge double room, a private bath and W.C. along with a connecting room with a private bath but no W.C.; or a second-floor suite that you reach through a salon that leads to the staircase and offers you a commodious double room, one with a double bed and one with a single bed. The scenic pleasures of Brittany—the island fortress of Mont St.-Michel, the druidical stones at Carnac, the walled town of Vannes—are moments away. The beaches of La Baule are 30 miles away. Except for a Continental breakfast, you won't eat at the château (there are a number of fine restaurants in the village), but you will want to have your afternoon tea there. Children under 12 are not allowed, leave your pets behind. Figure around $75 a day for the first-floor suite, and $50 a day for the second-floor double room.

Adventures Unlimited
117 E. 57th St.
New York, N.Y. 10022

A TENNIS VILLA IN THE CARIBBEAN

There aren't that many of them and it's tough to rent them during the peak seasons (Christmas week, February, and Easter week), but throughout the Caribbean, especially in Jamaica, there are a handful of private villas with tennis courts right on the grounds. Not all of them have easy access to the beach, but nearly all of them have swimming pools, and, as with all rented villas in the Caribbean, your rental fee includes a service staff— generally a maid, cook and gardener. Weekly prices during the season start at around $1500 for a three-bedroom villa in Jamaica. Larger, more elaborate villas run around $2000. During the off season, rates drop by about 40%. To find out about villa rentals, check the real estate section of your Yellow Pages, or contact the tourist office of the island you're interested in.

THE ANTI-STRESS "CURE" AT BADEN-BADEN

An eight-day smorgasbord of thermal baths, massages, and stuff like that run by a West German stress specialist named Dr. Werner Hess. It costs around $240 and includes everything but the plane fare to Baden-Baden. Check the West German tourist office for details.

German National Tourist Office
630 Fifth Ave.
New York, N.Y. 10026

A WEEK AT A PLUSH SPA

A place like the Golden Door, in Escondido, California, or Elizabeth Arden's Maine Chance in Scottsdale, Arizona. There are differences in each place but the basic regimen is pretty much the same. You get facials, body massages, heat treatments, scalp treatments, manicures, pedicures, customized exercises, yoga instruction, herbal wraps. You can go to these places to lose weight or gain weight, to tone yourself up, to get a "new look." Prices at the Maine Chance, which was the nation's pioneer beauty spa and remains to this day the best known and most prestigious, range from $1000 to $1200 for a week, everything included except the 15% service charge. The Golden Door gets $1250, plus a 15% service charge, and has special weeks for men at the same price.

Maine Chance
Camelback Road
Scottsdale, Arizona 85251

The Golden Door
Box 1567
Escondido, Cal. 92025

A LUXURY SUITE ON THE QE II

Weighing in at 66,000 gilded tons, Cunard's *QE II* is the only really *big* cruise ship left on the seas, a third again larger than her nearest rival. No other ship is as fast, as comfortable, or as grand, and no other travel experience approaches the *QE II* in terms of hassle-free luxury. Each year, the *QE II* slates one extended cruise (as well as some minor ones) that lasts around 90 days. It takes you around the world or something roughly approximate. Try to work yourself into one of the two new luxury bi-level suites: the Trafalgar or the Queen Anne. The Trafalgar presents an interior motif inspired by the quarters of Admiral Nelson when he was calling the shots on the flagship *Victory*. The suite is two stories, and you have a 15 × 18 foot veranda on each level. The furnishings are teak, the beds are admiral-sized. Across the hall is the Queen Anne suite, which is similar in structure to the Trafalgar suite but furnished in period pieces. Each suite accommodates four, but there's no reason that two people can't occupy them as well. As a resident of either suite, you are served by two stewards and a stewardess, at least one of whom is on call 24 hours. (They sleep in quarters adjacent to the suites.) You also get a chance each day to plan your next day's meal with the maître d' and can order whatever you desire in the way of caviar, champagne, or Bordeaux wines: there are no limits. The price for each suite is $150,000 for the 90-day trip. Other luxury suites average $35,000 a person. If you wish to slum it, there are accommodations available for $9000 a person. In any event, when you take a *QE II* cruise, everything—everything!—is taken care of for you from the moment you step onto the ship until the moment your bags are loaded into the taxi back at the pier.

CHARTERING YOUR OWN YACHT

Where to start? Why not at the top? For $45,000 a week, you and as many as 11 of your friends can charter *La Belle Simone,* the floating palace originally built by William Levitt, the builder, and named after his wife. The largest yacht built since 1972, she sails out of the Mediterranean and will take you in and out of the Riviera's tonier marinas. Around 250 feet long, she has a teak deck, can cruise at 16 knots, and has a 4500 mile range. The main suite (you'll have to draw straws or flip coins) has a salon deck, a 20 × 30 foot bedroom, his and her bathrooms, a sitting room, and a cedar closet. Marble baths and gold fixtures separate the remaining cabins from the ordinary. *La Belle* has her own swimming pool, an elevator, a stereo system, a television set, and two grand pianos. It takes a crew of 20 to run the thing, but they know how to keep out of your way. Your weekly price includes only the yacht and the crew. Everything else—the food, the fuel, the wine, the docking fees—are extra. Figure at least $12,000 more.

You can do it for less. A 15-day cruise through the Mediterranean on a medium-sized yacht housing eight people generally costs between $600 and $700 a person, everything included. A similar cruise through the Greek islands runs around $600, but the air fare from the U.S. will be a little more. Caribbean charters are all over the place: as little as $450 a couple for a week if you want to crew the boat yourself (food is included) to around $750 a person for a 15-day jaunt on a medium-sized yacht with six passengers and a small crew. The economic guidelines are fairly basic: the bigger and fancier the boat, the more it's going to cost. Your best approach, if you're interested, is to pick up one of the boating magazines and check out the ads. You can also explore the *Yellow Pages* under Boat Charters. It's a big business. You should have no trouble getting something organized.

A GREEK ISLAND TO YOURSELF FOR A WEEK

It's not Míkonos or Dílos or Naxos, but it *is* a Greek island in the middle of the cluster of islands south of Piraeus known as the Cyclades. A seven-hour cruise from Piraeus, the island has 10 verdant acres, a villa with three bedrooms, and a four-bed guest cottage. You can rent it for $800 a day. If you want the 55-foot motor cruiser (it sleeps six) to ferry you to the disco palaces of Paros and Naxos, figure an additional $300 a day.

> Adventures Unlimited
> 117 E. 57th St.
> New York, N.Y. 10022

A WEEK AT A JAPANESE RYOKAN

Pardon the redundancy. The only ryokans *are* Japanese. Traditional Japanese inns, they combine a foyer, living room, tea ceremony room, veranda, bath, and lavatory. You sleep on a *futon*—a floor mattress—take Japanese-style baths, receive Japanese-style massages, wear Japanese-style clothes, and partake of Japanese-style food in your ryokan. Finding a ryokan in Japan is as easy as finding a McDonald's in suburban Chicago. About 80,000 of them are spread throughout the country, although only 1300 are registered by the government and are considered top drawer. One of the most famous is Kikka-so (Chrysanthemum Villa), which General MacArthur commandeered as a top staff villa after the war. He did not return. The average price for a day's stay in a ryokan is between $80 and $100, which includes breakfast and dinner.

YOUR OWN PRIVATE RAILROAD CAR FOR A CROSS-COUNTRY TRIP

Originally, it was the mid-train lounge on the Broadway Limited. That was in 1949. Today it's the Lionel-Ives, a sleeper-buffet-lounger railroad car privately owned by an Amtrak executive named Larry Battley, who rents it out for scheduled Amtrak trips. It has six bedrooms, a galley with a refrigerator and light cooking facilities, and a lounge that holds 27 people. If you have the time, rent it for Amtrak's cross-country 8000-mile, 16-day trip, which starts in Philadelphia and heads northward to New York and then on the northwest route through Glacier National Park to Seattle, and then back to Philadelphia by the Southern route. You and no more than nine of your friends can rent the car, with an attendant (he sleeps in one of the bedrooms) for around $15,325. This includes two meals a day, breakfast and lunch, plus about $300 in booze. You take your dinner in the train's dining car—a good place to meet some people you'd like to invite into the lounge. About three-quarters of that price goes to Amtrak for mileage fees, etc. The rest is for the car itself, attendant, food, and drinks.

Larry Battley
2780 N. Quincy St.
Arlington, Va. 22207

A VACATION IN THE BUFF

It's all organized and legit. You swim at a government-approved nude beach with people who like the natural life. A number of companies are now organizing such tours. One of them is V.I.B. in New York. A typical eight-day/seven-night vacation in the buff in St. Maarten runs around $325, which includes air fare but no meals. Please don't dance naked in the aisles. Check your travel agent. Or call (800) 221-2622.

THE WORKS AT ELIZABETH ARDEN

Women who get it with reasonable regularity swear that it's better than a visit with a psychiatrist. On an hourly basis, it's cheaper. There are three basic packages. The "Miracle Morning" package—the most popular—buys you a body massage, facial, hair styling, and manicure. It lasts four hours and costs around $58. The "Maine Chance" offers everything the "Miracle Morning" offers but throws in an exercise class, some steam room time, a pedicure, and a nice salad platter for lunch. It takes 5½ hours and runs around $84. The "Visible Difference" involves a hair consultation, facial, hair styling, manicure, and make-up lesson. It takes four hours and costs around $72.

TWO WEEKS AT AN ASHRAM

No question, the cheapest way to stay. Virtually none of the religious retreats in India have any fees as such. What you do is leave a donation—anywhere from $25 to $100 is the average—when you leave. Typical of the kind of place you might want to decompress at is Hardwar, a Hindu religious center 140 miles northeast of New Delhi, where the Ganges River enters the Plains. Hardwar is to Hindus what Mecca is to Moslems. The accommodations could be niftier. You'll sleep on the floor (maybe a mat), and the food you eat will be strictly vegetables. There are no packaged tours. You have to take care of the air fare on your own. It costs around $800 to fly from New York to New Delhi. The round-trip plane fare from New Delhi to Hardwar is $10.

Journey World
527 Madison Ave.
New York, N.Y. 10022

A GLORIOUS WEEK IN PARIS

In April, of course. You can old-guard it with a suite at the Ritz—around $400 a day—or get a lesson in Louis XV and XVI at the Plaza-Athenée for roughly the same price. Dinner every night—pressed duck at Tour d'Argent; sautéed salamander at Chez Denis, where *New York Times* food editor Craig Claiborne and a friend managed to get rid of $4000 at a single setting; steak dumas at Lasserre—should average between $90 and $120 as long as you don't get too particular about the year of your Haut Brion. A night at Régine's should run around $150 for two, if you stay long enough and drink enough. A typically Parisian orgy—you have to bring your own partner—at a well-known place called Le Marronnier runs around $35 per person. Stay away from the big splashy nightclubs. Do a lot of walking along the Seine. Zip down to Versailles and back. Have a picnic in the Bois de Boulogne. Budget about $4000 for the week, not counting your air fare or any shopping.

WHEELING AND DEALING

PRODUCING YOUR OWN BROADWAY SHOW

The first question is whether you want your name associated with a musical or a straight play. The next question is how lavish and complicated a production is it you want it to be. The least expensive successful show in recent Broadway memory was *The Subject Was Roses,* a one-set, three-character play that came in at about $100,000. That was in the mid-1960's. The same play today would be much closer to $200,000. The most expensive bomb in recent memory was *Hellzapoppin,* the Jerry Lewis musical. Alexander Cohen produced it for a figure said to be in excess of $1.3 million. *1600 Pennsylvania Avenue,* the musical disaster for which Alan Lerner wrote the lyrics and Leonard Bernstein contributed the music, cost $1 million and bombed. *Sly Fox,* which brought George C. Scott back to Broadway, cost around $300,000, but would have been less with a less-prominent name. A safe minimum for a major musical these days is around $700,000. For a straight play, if the cast isn't the size of the

Red Army and you don't need 4000 carpenters to build the sets, you can probably get something mounted for around $250,000. What kills you in the end are the contracts you have to make with your creative people. Producers don't wield as much power as you might think. Get it into your head to ax your director before the show has opened, for instance, and chances are you'll have to keep him on the payroll for a long, long time. There is also a limit to what you can do when it comes to casting the show, so if you're hoping that your new role will enhance your sex life, you may be disappointed. Then again, you get to set up an office (and can hire whatever *secretaries* you want) and in the event the show takes off, you will be one of the most sought-after individuals in New York.

OWNING YOUR OWN SUMMER THEATER

You figure your expenses along two lines: one, what it will take to buy the theater; two, what it will take to run the theater each season. The going price for any reasonably established summer theater in the United States today is between $150,000 and $200,000. Once you own it, you either bring in packaged shows or mount your own shows with your own company. Importing a season of packaged shows—Billy Carter and Zsa Zsa Gabor in *West Side Story*, Ed McMahon in *Fiddler on the Roof*, etc., will probably mean a budget of $250,000 to $300,000 a season. Setting up everything on your own, once you have finished paying for the rights, scenery, programs, and advertising, insurance, and bribes to fire inspectors, will run between $150,000 and $200,000.

A McDONALD'S FRANCHISE

Figure about $225,000, at least $100,000 in cash. That's to open the doors. The waiting list for franchises is more than two years long. You have to open the place wherever they tell you to.

SPECULATING WITH OIL LEASES

The easiest way is to get in on what might best be called the Federal Government oil lease sweepstakes. And that's what it is, really—a sweepstakes. Each month, in 10 western states, the government raffles off land that may or may not have oil on it. Entering the drawing costs $10. If you win you pay the first year's rent—50 cents an acre. (Be careful; some plots are upwards of 2500 acres.) Should you win and should the land be in an area that the pros think has good oil potential, you can either sell off the rights to an oil company (average price, $100 an acre) or wildcat the land yourself. For more information, contact the Bureau of Land Management, an agency of the Interior Department.

A SEAT ON THE NEW YORK STOCK EXCHANGE

Less and less each year. At one time, seats were selling in excess of $200,000. In 1977 seats were sold for less than $90,000.

YOUR OWN PROFESSIONAL SPORTS
FRANCHISE

Unfortunately, it's not as much fun as it used to be with the advent of players' agents and ungrateful superstars and tougher tax laws that make it harder to write off your losses, but owning your own professional team still holds enough appeal to enough people that it's pretty much a seller's market in most sports. What you have to pay is mainly a matter of what sport you want to get involved in and which franchise holds your fancy. A new franchise in the National Football League will run you around $16 million, and that's just for the *franchise:* everything else— players' salaries, stadium space, etc., is extra. If you want an established team, figure closer to $20 million. The average major league baseball team today is probably worth around $12 million, more if it happens to be the Cincinnati Reds. George Steinbrenner and his group spent $10 million for the New York Yankees in the early 1970's. Bob Short spent $9.4 million for the now-defunct Washington Senators in 1968. Hockey? Well, Roy Boe spent around $10 million to buy the New York Islanders in the early 1970's, but you could probably get a World Hockey Association franchise for around $1.5 million. The only problem is remembering their nicknames. Professional basketball teams these days are valued between $7 million and $9 million, which some people consider excessive given the fact that hardly any of them turn a profit. A franchise in the World Team Tennis League is now said to be valued at around $1 million, but you could probably buy most teams for around $750,000. Sponsoring a Little League team, at last glance, was around $50.

BECOMING A BROADWAY ANGEL

The odds are better in Vegas, but at least you get invited
to opening night and can go to the party at Sardi's and
wait for the reviews. Pieces in Broadway shows are
generally sold in units of $1000 for musicals, less for
comedies and dramas. A couple of things to bear in mind
about investing in Broadway: first, more than 75% of the
shows produced on Broadway never pay back their
investors the full amount; second, even if the show
makes a profit, the investors usually split it with the
producer. On the other hand, investors get paid back
their initial stake before the producer takes any profit
(although the producer charges a fee). There's always a
chance; if you had invested $10,000 in *Oklahoma!,* you'd
be $0.5 million richer today.

A SWISS BANK ACCOUNT

Many Swiss banks will open up an account for you for as
little as $1000. The top banks won't consider you for less
than $25,000. Interest is less than 4%. The bank withholds
30% for Swiss taxes, unless you declare the account on
your own return.

The big advantage of having your money stashed in a
numbered Swiss account is secrecy. There are banks in
the United States that will reveal the contents of your
bank account to anybody from your local garbage man
on up. Swiss banks take the position, generally, that the
amount of money you have in your account is nobody's
business but yours.

A MILLION DOLLARS' WORTH OF LIFE INSURANCE

It depends on whether you're talking straight term or something in an endowment policy, not to mention how old you are. Assuming you're 35, straight term insurance will run you around $2290 for the year. A really great endowment policy could run around $100,000.

YOUR OWN RACEHORSE

Breeding is all. For a nobody in a claiming race, not much at all: $3000 or $4000. A horse with the blood of Secretariat will probably run you around $250,000, with no way of telling, incidentally, how the horse will do in competition. The average price for horses auctioned each July at the select horse auction in Lexington, Kentucky is $40,000. The auction open to the public in September usually fetches an average $20,000 per horse. There are any number of ways of buying, from buying a mare in foal to buying a good mare, breeding her and then waiting two years or so to develop a horse worth racing.

YOUR OWN RESTAURANT

Nothing too elaborate. An average-sized place in an average-sized city. The rule of thumb most experienced restaurateurs use (and get used to the term, restaurateur, there is no "n") is about $3000 per seat. It can easily go higher, depending on who you get to design the place and what your designer chooses to put on the walls. Also, on what sort of cooking equipment you want for the kitchen. On average, a 150-seat restaurant should take about $500,000.

YOUR OWN STOCK TICKER

The basic wire ticker—that gives you a running account of all the day's transactions on whichever market you're interested in. For the New York Stock Exchange ticker, $148 a month, assuming there aren't any problems hooking into phone lines. To get the service, you simply apply to the Exchange. You need official approval, but for private individuals it's automatic.

A more exotic variation of the stock ticker is something called the Video Master, which is made by GTE. It's a small console with a 12-inch cathode-ray tube and what it does is to give you, on command, a lot of specific information (opening price, current price, etc.) about a lot of different stocks. You lease them and the price is around $425 a month.

A HOME GASOLINE PUMP

To spare you the indignities of cooling your heels at your local gas station when and if the Arabs decide to turn off the spigots again. Local zoning ordinances could be a problem, but from a purely mechanical standpoint, it's no big deal. All you need is a tank and a pump. The typical gas station uses a tank with a 20,000 gallon capacity. You could get by with a 2000 gallon capacity. Figure about $1100 for the tank and $1000 to have it installed underground. The pump shouldn't run you more than $4000. Buying in bulk should save you a few pennies off the normal pump price. Check with a local oil jobber in your area.

A GUARANTEED GOOD TABLE AT A GOOD RESTAURANT

About $20 as an initial investment and $5 each time thereafter. You pay the first $5 to the maître d' who seats you no matter where he seats you—even if it's in the men's room. When the meal is over, hand him another $5 on your way out and thank him. Within a day or so, go to the same place and repeat the procedure. This time, though, when you leave and are divesting yourself of another $5, inform the maître d' that you'll be calling him the next day for a reservation and would he make sure you get a nice table.

WILDCATTING YOUR OWN OIL WELL

It's not for dilettantes, but with oil fetching $11 a barrel and some wells disgorging 3000 barrels a day, it's not hard to figure out why in Texas, for example, there is a new well drilled on the average of one every seven minutes! The first thing you'll need is an oil lease—a piece of paper that gives you the right to drill for oil on land that somebody else owns, with the proviso that you will bestow upon the land owner a royalty—usually 12½%—of whatever riches you accumulate. The cost of the lease will vary according to the likelihood of there being oil under the ground. You could spend as little as $10 an acre or as much as $1000. Once your lease is squared away, you'll need a local geologist to set up a drilling strategy for you. On a percentage deal, you can get him for next to nothing. On a straight fee deal, figure $400 a day. Drilling crews charge by the foot—anywhere from $8 to $20 depending on the terrain, the accessibility, etc. This does not include what they call drilling mud—a pricey lubricant that fluctuates more than price of gold—and pipe casing, which runs between $2 and $4 a foot. Once the drilling starts, you'll need a logging crew—guys to come in, analyze the stuff coming out of the ground and tell how and when to "fracture"—set an underground explosion. Figure $1000 a day. Usually you'll know by between three days and a week whether you've struck black gold or not, by which time you'll have dug anywhere from 1000 to 2000 feet. If you get lucky, you'll need more equipment—a tank, a pump, piping, and you probably won't know for certain if the well will yield oil for years or will dry up in three days. On average, you can figure an investment of between $50,000 and $75,000 for a normal drilling situation, although you have to remember that there is no such thing as normal in the oil business. The odds of your coming up with a strike on a typical wildcat deal are about one in 10.

BELONGING

THE AUGUSTA NATIONAL GOLF CLUB

Possibly the toughest golf club to get into in the U.S., with a waiting list longer than the 14th hole. You don't get *proposed* here. You get *invited* to join. The initiation fee is around $12,000. Dues run around $1000 a year.

THE WEST SIDE TENNIS CLUB

Formerly the site of the U.S. Open, and no question, the best place to play tennis if you live in the New York area. The club has 48 courts, eight of them grass. The price, if you can get in, is $800 initiation (if you're male and over 30) with annual dues of $465. Men between 26 and 30 pay an initiation fee of $530 and dues of $305. Women over 30 pay a $700 initiation fee and $400 dues. Women between 26 and 30 pay $90 and $280. There are no court fees and no minimum restaurant charges. To get into the club, you have to be proposed by one member, seconded by another, and have to be acquainted with at least four members of the Membership Committee and three members of the Board of Governors.

INTERNATIONAL CHINESE SNUFF BOTTLE SOCIETY

Everybody who belongs to the International Chinese Snuff Bottle Society—and there are about 550 members—has a thing about Chinese snuff bottles. As a member, you get the quarterly journal and can attend the annual convention, which in past years has been in London and Washington. Dues are $25 a year.

International Chinese Snuff Bottle Society
2601 N. Charles St.
Baltimore, Md. 02178

THE PROCRASTINATORS' CLUB OF AMERICA

Founded in 1956, the Procrastinators' Club of America currently numbers around 3000, but according to its president, Lee Waas, "We have over half a million members except that most people haven't gotten around to joining us yet." Once a member, you receive a parchment License to Procrastinate that is suitable for framing, along with a membership card dated 1987. The club publishes a monthly newsletter a month late and urges members to become "inactive on a committee." There is a busy agenda of causes and trips: a Christmas party every June, a visit to a ski resort in July. The PCA's most important cause over the past 10 years has been a protest against the War of 1812. It was organized in 1967. There is now excited talk among club members to organize a campaign designed to grant voting rights to American women. The initial membership fee is $10, and the annual dues are $5. If you pay your dues on time, the club assesses you a 5% penalty. Write tomorrow for more details.

The Procrastinators' Club of America
1111 Broad St.
Philadelphia, Pa. 17011

THE NATIONAL ORGANIZATION OF SCRABBLE PLAYERS

If you don't mind wordy people, the National Organization of Scrabble Players could add a pleasant new dimension to your life. Joining entitles you to the bi-monthly newsletter and a membership card. The newsletter tells you about Scrabble tournaments in your area. The price is $5.

Scrabble Crossword Game Players, Inc.
Box N, 200 Fifth Ave.
New York, N.Y. 10010

THE METROPOLITAN OPERA GUILD

An associate membership is $15. A national membership is $20. The $20 membership entitles you to a year's subscription to *Opera News*. Both memberships entitle you to the yearly Metropolitan Opera guide. You also get a personalized membership card, reduced rates on back-stage tours, and a mail-order service that you can use to buy discount books, records, reproductions, etc.

Metropolitan Opera Guild
1865 Broadway
New York, N.Y. 10023

JIM SMITH SOCIETY

The membership requirements for this club are obvious: your name has to be James Smith. According to the President, Jim Smith, and the secretary, Jim Smith, membership includes Jim Smiths as far away as New Zealand. As a member you get a membership card, two Jim Smith wooden nickels, and four Jim Smith newsletters a year. Last year the Jim Smith Society held its convention in Las Vegas. A softball game—it's tough to tell the players even *with* a scorecard—highlights the annual meeting. Membership fee is $5. Dues are $5 annually.

Jim Smith Society
James H. Smith, Jr., President
2016 Miltown Rd.
Camp Hill, Pa. 17011

JOHN BIRCH SOCIETY

The 90,000 or so people who belong to the John Birch Society pay dues of $24 a year for women or $48 a year for men. Not everybody can belong. Right for details.

John Birch Society
395 Concord Ave.
Belmont, Mass. 02178

GETTING ON THE PREFERRED LIST AT RÉGINE'S, IN NEW YORK

Régine's eight international nightclubs are heavy numbers on the jet set hit parade. If she asks you—a pretty big if—you can become a "preferred" guest in the Manhattan Régine's. This means you get a card and can reserve a table in advance. It also means that you can get into the Paris, Monte Carlo, Rio and Bahia branches without a hassle. The price is $600 a year.

AN AIRLINE VIP CLUB

Time was you had to either *be* somebody or *know* somebody to join an airline VIP club and get to use the private lounges in airports, *get free drinks* and stuff like that. But a CAB crackdown changed all that. Today, if you want to join an airline VIP club, all you have to do is be willing to pay the dues, which average between $20 and $30 a year or between $250 and $300 a lifetime. If you're interested, contact the airline of your choice and they'll tell you how to go about it.

THE ROCK OF THE MONTH CLUB

The nicest thing about the Rock of the Month Club is that you can drop out anytime you like and rejoin anytime you like for no extra charge. An initial outlay of $4.50 entitles you to a monthly package ($3) of selected rocks, plus $1.50 for postage deposit.

Rock of the Month Club
3901 Pershing Drive
El Paso, Tex. 79903

THE BALD-HEADED MEN OF AMERICA

Again, the qualifications are obvious. The better-known members include Gerald Ford and Joe Garagiola. The initiation fee is $5 and there are no annual dues. As a member, you get a certificate, a membership card, and the organization's quarterly, which is called *Chrome-Dome*. The basic purpose of the club is to make you proud that you're bald. It is not necessary to take an oath against toupees.

Bald-Headed Men of America
Box "Bald"
211 N. King Ave.
Dunn, N.C. 28335

HAVING AN AFFAIR

A SUPERSTAR TO PERFORM AT YOUR DAUGHTER'S WEDDING

It can be done, but it's a touchy business and money isn't always the key. The main thing that any performer, particularly a singer, is worried about is making a fool out of himself. Don't expect Sinatra to sing "My Way" with a bunch of turkeys on the bandstand even if you're paying him $100,000. Once an entertainer doesn't have to worry about his back-up support, it next comes down to how well he (or she) knows you and what their normal club date fee is. A number of entertainers, as a favor, will come and perform for no charge, which is to say that when they're finished you show your appreciation by buying them a new Cadillac or else sticking fifty $100 bills in their pocket. This is why their *knowing* you or somebody who approaches them for you is so important—they figure you know how the game works. If you want to do it on a strict business basis, it helps to know what the going rates are. The really big names—the Johnny Carsons, the Chers, the Tom Jones, the John

Denvers, etc.—get paid between $200,000 and $250,000 a week in Las Vegas and figure their time is worth $50,000 a night, plus expenses. Lesser names—the Jerry Vails, the Peggy Lees—usually get around $50,000 a *week* in Las Vegas and might be receptive to offers in the $10,000 category. Most jazz names—Ramsey Lewis, Dave Brubeck, Bobby Short, Sarah Vaughn—are in the $3500 to $7000 bracket and are probably the easiest to hire. If possible, try *not* to deal with the agent. The first thing the agent will want to know is how much you have to spend. He'll then get you somebody who would have been delighted to work for half that fee. If you're consumed with the idea of bringing a big name to whatever affair you're involved with, try to work with an established booking agent.

A WEDDING CEREMONY ON WATER SKIS

The hard part is getting a minister, rabbi, priest, or justice of the peace who can stay on the skis long enough to make it official. (One good thing: it will be a short ceremony!) Not to worry. Cypress Gardens in Florida will arrange for everything: the boat, the marriage official, the driver, the gas, the music, the skis, and even flowers (water lilies, of course). What's more, they'll pay for everything, as long as you do it at Cypress Gardens. As of this writing, nobody has done it.

Cypress Gardens
P.O. Box 1
Cypress Gardens, Fla. 33880

A SKATING PARTY AT THE ROCKEFELLER CENTER SKATING RINK

Easily done but with one condition: you can only rent the rink from 11 P.M. to 10 A.M. (The rink is normally open during the season from 10:30 A.M. to 10:30 P.M.) You get the rink along with a staff of seven: the manager, a cloakroom person, two instructors—they charge individually ($6 per half-hour)—a couple of attendants who help to keep order, and somebody to rent skates. You're not allowed to bring in food. If you want to serve food, you have to deal with the adjacent restaurant. The price for the rink is $300 an hour. You get a dollar reduction—$2—on the normal skate renting fee.

Rockefeller Center Skating Rink
Rockefeller Center
New York, N.Y. 10020

RENTING AN ELEPHANT

A guest that everyone who comes to your party will remember. He (or she) will usually give rides or simply stand there and be big. Normally, you'll get the elephant for a couple of hours and unless there are severe logistical problems, you can figure around $750.

All Tame Animals
37 W. 57th St.
New York, N.Y. 10022

A PARTY AT A LANDMARK MANSION

Lyndhurst, in Tarrytown, N.Y. (Jay Gould's old place); Bell Grove, in Middleton, Va.; Chesterwood, in Stockbridge, Mass.; Cliveden, in Philadelphia; Decatur House in Washington, D.C.; Otlands, in Leesburg, Va.; the Phoe-Leighty House, in Mt. Vernon, Va.; Shadows-on-the-Teche, in New Iberia, La.; Woodlawn Plantation, in Mt. Vernon, Va.; the Woodrow Wilson house, in Washington, D.C. If you belong to a nonprofit club or group, you can rent any one of these National Trust Historic Properties for "official" functions. The fee ranges from $50 to $500, depending on the site and the nature of the event. Contact each place directly.

A FRENCH CHEF TO CATER YOUR BANQUET

Somebody with the right credentials: a *Guide Michelin* two- or three-star restaurant or a place of authority in one of the country's top restaurants. He'll plan the menu for you, select the wines, and even import the fresh foie gras for you, if it's the right time of year. Naturally, you will not quibble about the prices. Since there is no agency that books French chefs, you will have to deal direct. The average fee for a single banquet is $2000, plus expenses.

LESTER LANIN TO PLAY AT YOUR RECEPTION

No longer do New York society matrons call Lester Lanin on the phone to say: "Mr. Lanin, my daughter is three weeks old, and I want to sign you up for her coming-out party at the St. Regis when she's eighteen." Still, Lanin is in the music business, and producing the same smart society sound. His fees vary according to what sort of a shindig you're putting on. Also, where you live, who you are and, surprisingly, how much you can afford to pay. For a three-piece Lester Lanin orchestra at a wedding reception, Lanin will charge in the neighborhood of $450 and will make a brief appearance. If you live in Denver and want a 15-piece orchestra and Lanin to be there the whole time, figure around $15,000. A 12-piece Lester Lanin ensemble for a Chicago affair should run between $5000 and $8000.

> Lester Lanin Orchestras
> 157 W. 57th St.
> New York, N.Y. 10019

THE CYPRESS GARDENS WATER SHOW FOR YOUR BACKYARD POOL

Slow down. First of all, your pool has to be at least 60 feet long. And don't expect the tow-gliding act, where the guy on water skis with a kite on his back is towed by a boat until he reaches a height of about 500 feet and then glides back into the water. What you get is a scaled-down version of the Florida show: a cast of eight, including Corky the Clown doing his ramp jumping number and corps de water ballet. A one-day performance, excluding transportation, will run about $4500. If you have a river or large lake, they'll bring the whole show—Kiteman and all, 15 people—for around $8000.

Cypress Gardens
P.O. Box 1
Cypress Gardens, Fla. 33880

A PRIVATE FIREWORKS DISPLAY

Somebody in upstate New York had it done for a wedding a while back. It began with the usual—sky-rockets and flares and lots of noise—but it ended with a sign that had the names of the bride and groom framed in a heart, surrounded by colored shells flashing in the air. You can do it, too. You have to contact a local fireworks display company. Chances are, they'll want you to spend a minimum of $200. You figure additional costs roughly as follows: a fixed amount of insurance, around $50, and a fixed amount for the man who sets them off. Whatever is left over goes for the fireworks. The upstate New York wedding ran $1500.

RENTING OUT A BIG LEAGUE SPORTS ARENA

Prices and policies are all over the place. The Astrodome, in Houston, has a base fee: $125,000 against 17.5% of the gate, whichever is higher. It doesn't matter what you put in there. You supply all the personnel. Madison Square Garden, in New York, has two fees: one for nonprofit affairs, the other for profit enterprises. The nonprofit fee is $25,000 for the night, plus expenses. The place is yours from 8 A.M. until 2 A.M. the following morning. When profit is involved, the deal goes like this: $27,500 from Monday to Friday, plus expenses; $30,000 on the weekend. You also kick over 22% of any ticket-selling revenue in excess of $130,000. At the Louisiana Superdome, in New Orleans, it's mostly a matter of how much room you want and what you want to do. For a theatrical event that could draw, say, 95,000 people, you have to guarantee a minimum of $25,000 for the day against 15%, whichever is greater.

A FABULOUS GARY HANSEN CAKE

When West Coast heavies need a big cake for a big occasion, they generally seek out Gary Hansen. Some examples of past performance: (1) A 25-lb cake stuffed with lox and cream cheese, ordered by Liz Taylor ($250). (2) A 25-foot cake with 25 layers, made at four days' notice for Bob Hope's 25th anniversary television party ($5000). (3) A wedding cake with an entourage of 25 bridesmaids in the styling of Louis XV and his court, with the tiers separated by Louis XV chair legs. For the biggest gay wedding of 1976 ($1800).

The price of a Hansen cake depends basically on how big it is, what's in it, how much artwork is involved, and how many man-hours it takes to create and deliver it.

The ultimate cake? How about a five-tier job with an edible bas-relief which would depict scenes from pre-Vesuvian Pompeii. The nymph of spring—a real baby—could jump through dancing waterfalls, and you could have trees and shrubbery in the icing to lend the proper atmosphere. Along with swaying palms. Hansen's estimate: about $10,000, but he could do it better, he adds, for $20,000.

Gary Hansen Cakes
1060 S. Fairfax
Los Angeles, Cal. 90019

YOUR OWN RESORT FOR A WEEKEND

The Hyatt Resort on Palmetto Dunes, Hilton Head Island, South Carolina, can accommodate around 722 people. If you want the place for yourself, or want to go somewhere where you have personally invited 721 other people, the price is $286,125.

YOUR OWN AMUSEMENT PARK FOR THE DAY

Houston's Astroworld can be rented for the day for about $50,000. Check with Sakowitz.

Sakowitz
1111 Main St.
Houston, Tex. 77002

SHADY DEALINGS

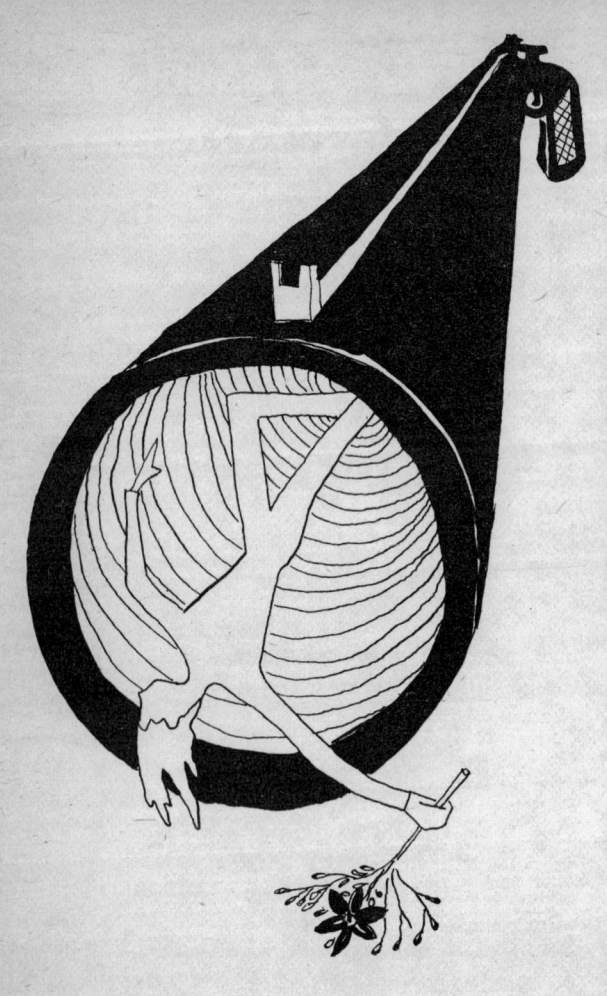

GETTING SOMEBODY ROUGHED UP

It is less expensive, but more difficult, to get somebody roughed up than to get somebody killed. Most of the better work that gets done in this area takes the form of "favors" to a friend, which is to say there are few contract men in the roughing up field. Still, there are some general criteria. If the person you want roughed up isn't too big or too dangerous or too famous and if you just want him shoved around and scared a little bit (taking a guy down to a waterfront and leaving him there is usually an effective strategy), figure around $200. More specialized work—a broken leg or thumb, etc.—calls for a more specialized talent, as much as $500 perhaps. There was a time when a lot of the men who did this kind of work were off-duty cops, but the pattern is changing. Your best entree is to go through a private detective, although you may have to contact several before you can get a guy to make the right connection for you. In the meantime, if you're booking somebody on your own, choose with care. There's always the chance the clown will turn around and blackmail you.

GETTING SOMEBODY KILLED

The economics of murder by hire hinge primarily on how well known the prospective victim is and how much you want it to look like an accident. If you don't care how the murder is done and if the person you want done away with is not the sort of person who's going to have bodyguards or whose death is going to make a big splash in the newspapers, you can probably find somebody to do it for as little as $300. That's what a typical junkie in a typical American slum will ask for, although you can't really expect much in the way of a guarantee. They are, after all, amateurs. Getting a seasoned pro will run you a minimum of $5000, which is for a basically uncomplicated situation. Little risk. No headlines. No special attempt to make it look like an accident. In other words, a simple hit. Introduce complications and the price goes up. The Jablonski murder fund was said to be $20,000. A Kentucky man was reportedly offered $500,000 to kill Martin Luther King, Jr. The killing of investigative reporter Don Bolles reportedly involved a $50,000 payment, but for three killings. Forget the *Yellow Pages*. The only way to handle it is to find somebody who knows somebody who knows somebody in the underworld.

BRIBING A COP

It's always risky—especially in California where the cops bring a dangerous degree of integrity to their work—but, generally speaking, if it's a very minor offense, like a traffic violation, and if the cop is by himself and has no reason to suspect you as a "plant," a $20 bill is standard. People well versed in this sort of thing keep a $20 bill folded alongside their driver's license, which explains why, in many states, the cop will ask you to take the license *out* of the wallet before you hand it to him. The way to get around this, if you want, is to have the $20 bill accidentally fall out of the wallet as you're pulling out the license. The cop will either get the idea or he won't.

A PHONY DRIVER'S LICENSE

With a fictitious name and address on it. Made to order on the same kind of typewriter that turns out the real thing. A basic tool in the kit of a bum-check artist. From $50 to $200.

AN ILLEGAL U.S. PASSPORT

The blackmarket price for a U.S. passport is said to be as much as $5000.

A SATURDAY NIGHT SPECIAL

A handgun, not a television show. On the street in most big cities, you can get them for around $50, but you can't be sure that the thing won't blow up in your face. When the heat is on, the price goes up to $100.

BUYING HOT MERCHANDISE

If you have to pay more than a third of the normal wholesale cost, you're being overcharged and, chances are, the stuff might not even be stolen. Clothes are the safest buy: they're impossible to trace. Cars are the chanciest.

DEALING WITH A LOAN SHARK

Dealing with your local loan shark is not as hairy a business as you might think from watching police shows on the tube. Loan sharking is illegal, of course, but the men who engage in it tend to be surprisingly flexible, much more so, in some cases, than the typical bank. There are two forms of loans: (1) a straight percentage loan; and (2) a "pay down" loan. On a straight percentage loan, you pay anywhere from 3% to 5% of the principal each week for as long as the loan is outstanding. So, a $2000 loan over a five-week period at 5% would run you about $500 in interest or, as everyone calls it, "vigorish"—that is, 25%. The longer the loan is outstanding, the more interest you end up paying. Use the figures cited above over a six-month period, and you'll end up paying more than double your principal in interest. The "pay down" loan works differently. You start out with a fixed time period—13 weeks, say—and you pay both the principal and the vigorish back on a weekly basis. For a $1000 loan, at 3%, you'll pay $100 a week for 13 weeks, but you can't pay less. If all you can manage is the interest—$30—you pay that and the time period is extended a week.

What if you can't meet the payments? Well, you normally don't have to worry about getting your legs broken or facial features rearranged or being thrown through a window (a loan shark, like any other business-man, is fussy about his image and nobody is anxious to scare off potential borrowers), although the possibility is always there. In extreme cases, a loan shark will do his best to scare you, but as long as he feels you're not taking advantage of his good nature you can sleep reasonably easy. (Although the interest meter keeps ticking away.) Since loan sharks do not advertise in the *Yellow Pages*, you have to be introduced to one. Gamblers are a good source for contacts.

MARIJUANA

In the good old days, an ounce of dependable Jamaican or Colombian grass ran from $15 to $20. At last look, the asking price in some circles was close to $100 and as much as $350 an ounce for the "Thai sticks" that used to sell for $20 during the Vietnam War. The reason for this inflationary spiral is that richer people are now smoking the stuff. The cheapest place to buy marijuana is on a college campus, where it sells among friends for between $15 and $60. An ounce of grass yields about 10 joints.

COCAINE

Unless you're a dealer or have a lot of cocaine-sniffing friends, you're probably going to buy cocaine by the gram, and the cost will invariably depend on the avail-able supply. In the U.S., a gram of cocaine—good for between four and six snorts—will run you anywhere from $25 to $75. An ounce of the stuff ranges from $1200 to

$2000. In Mexico, you can get good cocaine for $4 a gram and $50 an ounce, but if you get caught trying to sneak it across the border, it may cost your friends a lot more than that to get you out of jail.

A HIT OF LSD

Anywhere from $1 to $3. A lot cheaper if you buy it bulk.

ADOPTING A CHILD ILLEGALLY

Most illegal adoptions are handled through lawyers who act as a conduit between the woman having the child and the couple who wants it. Getting a baby in this way is against the law, but once the deal is settled, problems rarely arise. The fee is generally between $5000 and $9000, and, in some cases, much higher.

AN ARSONIST

It depends whether you're in the market for a pro or for somebody off the street to throw some gasoline and a match. For small jobs where there is little danger to the arsonist, $100 is usually enough to find a willing torch. For a big job in which heavy insurance money is at stake, you'll need a professional. He will want a large chunk of money in front and a percentage of the insurance, just like a lawyer. A torch named Merrill Klein, who was once known as the dean of contract arsonists, used to get 15%.

HOT CREDIT CARDS

For a gas card, around $10. For an American Express or Bank card, around $25. The hotter the card, of course (how recently it's been taken), the more valuable it is.

COMMUNICATING

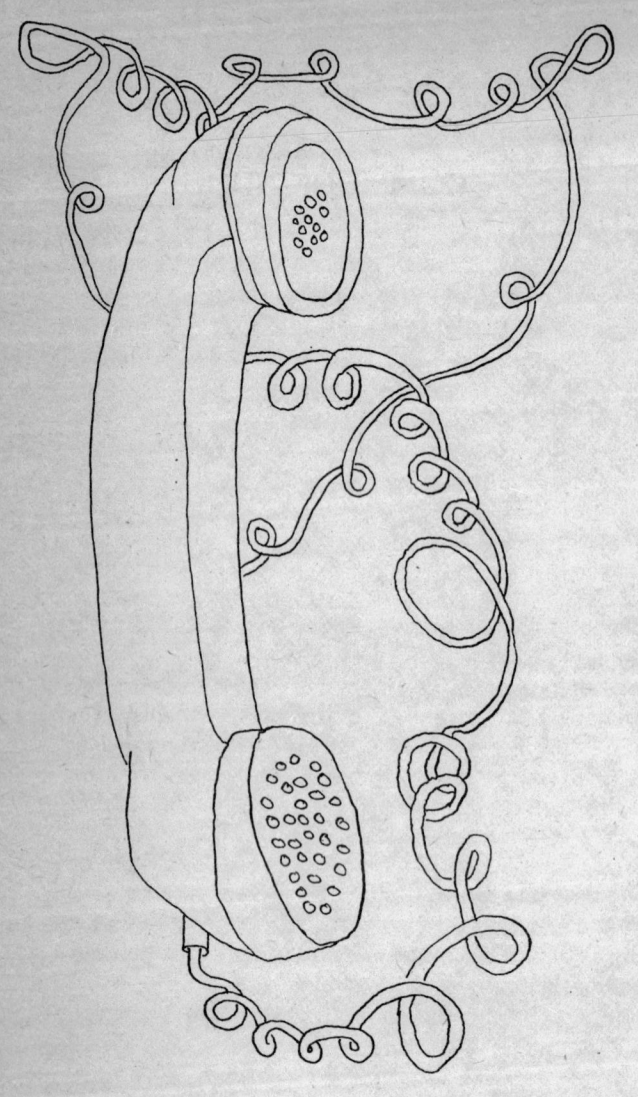

A PHONE IN YOUR CAR

It's called a mobile phone, and the price depends on how wide a calling range you need to cover and the policy of your local phone company. If you live in Connecticut and want stateside service, you pay around $130 for installation plus $88.50 a month. This entitles you to 60 minutes of conversation (that's minutes, not calls!). For every additional minute, figure 20¢. There are no dialers on this type of mobile phone. You simply flash the operator when you want to make a call, or the phone rings when someone wants you. If you want a dial unit—called roamer service—to initiate and receive calls out of state or within state, the installation fee is around $218 and the monthly fee is around $134 for 60 minutes, plus normal long-distance rates and an additional 20¢ for each additional minute.

YOUR OWN WATS LINE

WATS stands for Wide Area Telephone Service. If you have the service, you can make an unlimited number of long-distance calls within a specific area for a fixed price. WATS is one-directional. You can get "in" service—an 800 number (see below)—or "out" service. You can get both. Prices vary from state to state. On the average, it will cost you between $50 and $60 for the extra phone. (You could have an extra button put on your existing phone, but it would cost more.) From here it's a question of how many calls you expect to make. For up to 10 hours a month— low volume—you pay around $250 a month and approximately $17 to $20 for each additional hour. For a high-volume WATS, monthly fees average $1600 or so for around 240 hours, plus $4 to $5 per hour overtime. If you want a WATS line for specific areas, prices vary, but it's so complicated you'd better talk it over with your local phone representative.

AN AUTOMATIC DIALER FOR YOUR PHONE

What it does is dial frequently called numbers for you automatically. Prices vary according to local phone company policy. Figure around $25 to install it, and $15 a month for the privilege of owning one.

YOUR OWN TELEX MACHINE

It's cheaper, in the long run, than telephone or cable and you have a written record of what you've said. The only catch is the only other people you can correspond with are fellow Telex owners. A basic Telex machine will run you around $2000. If you don't mind a lot of noise, you can get one without the cover for around $1650. Figure $25 a month or so to Western Union for line service. Check the business machine section of your *Yellow Pages,* or a Western Union office.

A CONFERENCE CALL

A conference call is any call involving three or more parties in different places. Presently, you can arrange a call for 30 people around the world. To set it up, you dial 0 and ask the operator to get you the conference operator. You give her the numbers you want to call, and she gives you the word on the price. Then you brew some coffee or read a magazine until she calls back and tells you everybody is ready. (If you're calling 30 people, you could probably read a good slice of *War and Peace.*) Some typical prices: A four-station call between Los Angeles, Miami, Chicago, and New York runs around $8.50 for the first three minutes and $1.75 for each additional minute. If you live in Kansas City and want to set up a conference call between yourself and your sister in Paris, your brother in London, your uncle in Nairobi, your judo instructor in Tokyo, and your aunt in Melbourne, figure $37.50 for the first three minutes and $10.70 for each additional minute.

YOUR OWN VIDEOTAPING SYSTEM

To tape your own video productions, you need three basic pieces of equipment: a camera, recorder, and

monitor to play it back on. For something very funda-
mental and not too versatile, you can probably get into
the ballgame for around $1300 or $1400. What you get is a
half-inch black-and-white camera that comes with one
lens but has no viewfinder, a standard recorder (it will
also tape shows right off the tube), and a nine-inch
monitor. From this point on, it's all a matter of what
features you want and whether you tape in black-and-
white or color. A good half-inch black-and-white camera
with a viewfinder, zoom lens, microphone, and tripod
runs around $900. Additional lenses run from $90 or so up
to $900 for a motorized zoom. Simple recorders start at
$900 for black-and-white. Something you can edit with
will run around $1250. Monitors start at $180 for the small
one. A 17-inch job should run closer to $300.

Get into color, and costs start to escalate. The camera
alone is going to cost around $4000, whether you go half
or three-quarter inch. Color recorders start at $2000 or so.
A monitor runs from $300 for a six-inch unit to $1400 for a
17-inch job loaded with special features. Cassettes run
from $12 to $25 depending on how long they run and
whether you want black-and-white or color. A half-hour
black-and-white tape in half-inch runs around $12. A 60-
minute color tape for a three-quarter-inch unit is around
$25. Shop around. There are lots of discounts in the field.

MAKING SURE THAT NOBODY "BUGS" YOU

You have reason to suspect that somebody—your wife,
your husband, your ex-partner, the CIA, the FBI, your
competitors, your tennis pro, Richard Nixon: somebody—
is snooping on you. Tapping your phone, maybe. Or

taping your conversations. Surveillance paraphernalia is more sophisticated than ever, but countersurveillance paraphernalia is getting just as sophisticated. A standoff. Here's a sampling of what you can get.

A Basic Tap Alert: it looks like a fancy cigar box and sits on your desk. In the middle of it is a digital readout that tells you at a glance if anybody has either put a tap on the line or picked up an extension phone. It works on a voltage measurement principle. Around $550.

A Bug Alert: a pocket-sized device that tells you by means of a light or meter whether somebody in the room you happen to be in discussing business has a hidden microphone or tape recorder. What you do is excuse yourself from the meeting about five minutes after it's started, head for the john and check out the alert to see if anything is shaking. Around $1000.

A Telephone Number Decoder: you connect it to whatever phones in your house or office you want and it keeps a running record of which numbers are dialed, when they were dialed, and how long the conversations lasted. About $4000.

A Wiretap Defeat System: a jazzed-up version of the bug alert which not only alerts you to the fact that someone is tapping your line but enables you to kill the tap or, if you want, control the information you want the tapee to hear. When one switch is on, the snooper hears what you're saying. When another switch is activated, he can't hear. Around $2700.

A Line Tap Locater: in the event you want to pinpoint the exact location of a telephone line tap up to 50,000 feet away. Around $24,000.

The Ultimate: an overall system of bug detectors that feeds into a console with 18 separate monitoring units. Ideal for the compleat paranoiac. You hire a staff to man it full time and you afford yourself the best around-the-clock anti-surveillance protection that money can buy. About $28,000.

Communication Control Systems
605 Third Ave.
New York, N.Y. 10016

LIFE, DEATH, AND MARRIAGE

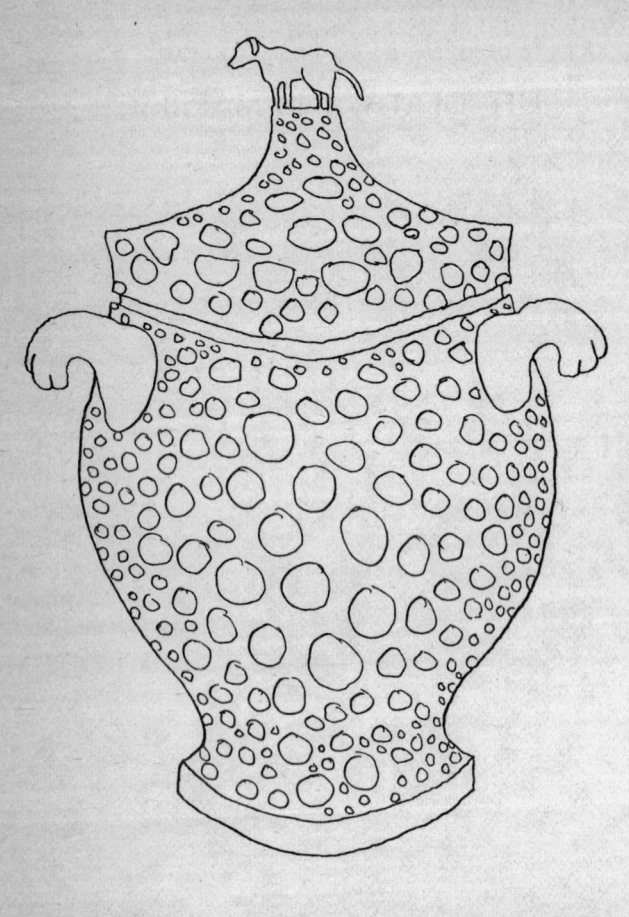

A WEDDING CEREMONY AT FOREST LAWN

Why not? It's a dying institution, anyway. The Forest Lawn Cemetery in Glendale, California (there are, by the way, four Forest Lawns in California), offers you a choice of six chapels for the exchanging of nuptial vows. In addition to the chapel, they supply the organist, wedding hostess, and uniformed attendant. You bring the minister and the flowers. The fee is $60.

A GITTINGS WEDDING PORTRAIT

The thing that makes a Gittings wedding portrait a little different from the sort of work of the photographer who lives around the corner from you is what they do after the photograph is taken. The Gittings process involves a dye transfer that is bonded onto canvas. Prices start at $135, which buys you a basic 8 × 10 inch color portrait. A

225

40 × 60 inch monster that goes through a four-stage process, all by hand, is $3350. Lots of variations in between.

Gittings Wedding Portrait
2436 E. Camelback Rd.
Phoenix, Ariz. 15026

AN AUTHENTIC COLONIAL WEDDING

The way they would have done it in George and Martha's time—or a close facsimile thereof. You arrange it through the Colonial Williamsburg foundation and here's how it works. You and your would-be groom (or bride) rent a small individual colonial home in Colonial Williamsburg (between $75 to $100 a night). You can have the ceremony right in the parlor, hold a reception on the terrace of the nearby Williamsburg Lodge and then return to the house for an Early American honeymoon. A two-hour reception at the Williamsburg Lodge for 50 people will run you upwards of $500. This buys you costumed waiters serving food (hors d'oeuvres) and drink of the period. You get fish house punch, bite-sized ham biscuits, crab legs, raw oysters, barbecued baby spareribs, pecan tarts, and assorted pastries. A colonial wedding cake—fruit cake with marzipan roses—comes with the reception. For a costumed balladeer to sing and play the lute for two hours, figure around $50 and don't expect him to know any Neil Diamond tunes. For a string ensemble to favor you with 18th century minuets, figure $150 for two hours. You can get the wedding gown made in Williamsburg, too. Figure around $350.

Banquet Office
Colonial Williamsburg
Williamsburg, Va. 23185

A DIVORCE

When there are no kids, no house, and nothing of real
value to hassle over, a married couple who wants to call
it a day should be able to do it for less than $300. You
have to shop around for a lawyer willing to clear only
$250 on the deal. Complicated divorces involving matri-
monial lawyers get you into the $1500 to $2500 bracket
(for each party), with the understanding that if the case
gets messy and winds up in court, the price goes up. For a
lawyer in Louis Nizer's stable, figure $5000 in advance.

A CUSTOM-ORDERED CHILD

You would like your child to carry the genes of a Nobel
Prize scientist, a pro football player, a beautiful actress: it
can be arranged. Not many people know about it, but
sperm banks in many parts of the country keep on file
specimens of sperm that have been donated anony-
mously by prominent people. The names of the donors
are kept secret, but the characteristics, physical and
mental, are kept on file. Be careful. You could wind up
with a girl who looks like Joe Namath and throws a pass
like Liv Ullman. You have to order through a gynecologist. The price is around $35.

A HEDGE AGAINST A VASECTOMY

You never know. That's why a lot of men who have undergone vasectomies have taken out some insurance of sorts by storing some of their live sperm in a sperm bank. Does it work? Well, studies have shown that modern-day freezing and storage methods have a negligible effect on the fertility level of the semen. Some loss of potency takes place, about 10%, but there are something like 50 million spermatozoa in each cubic centimeter of semen. It only takes one to score, so the odds are in your favor. Fees: most sperm banks charge $55 for the first specimen—about 3 cc (and 150 million spermatozoa)—and $50 for each specimen thereafter. Sperm banks recommend a minimum of three samples. Once surrendered, there is a storage fee of $25 a year—cheaper if you do it on a five-year plan.

DONATING YOUR GENES TO POSTERITY

Actually, they pay you. The average sperm bank shells out $20 for a sperm specimen. There's only one catch. Since the life span of sperm is notoriously short, you have to produce it for them on the premises.

AN AIRBORNE BURIAL

An organization in California called the Flying Funeral Directors of America will take your ashes or those of a loved one up in an airplane, scatter them to the wind, say a prayer, and supply a certificate giving the date, time, and latitude and longitude at which the burial ceremony took place. The price is $25. There are no movies.

YOUR PET CREMATED

Most major cities have people who specialize in cremating pets. The price depends on the size of the departed loved one and the quality of the urn that will house the ashes. Figure between $40 and $70.

KEEPING YOUR BODY FROZEN ONCE YOU DIE

It is altogether possible that years from now medicine will unearth a way to repair whatever it is you may die from. Cryonics—the freezing of the dead—is a strategy designed to exploit the possibility. The process involves replacing your blood with antifreeze and then placing your corpse in a capsule that is periodically replenished with nitrogen. Comes the discovery to restore your life, you get a transfusion and emerge from the experience, presumably, looking no worse for wear than the day you shucked off the mortal coil. The price for cryonics keeps going up. At last look it was around $50,000, payable in advance. Interested parties should contact their local cryonics society. Dress warm.

CULTURE MONGERING

THE PASSION PLAY AT OBERAMMERGAU

About 300 years ago, a plague that ravaged central Europe miraculously spared a tiny, scenic Bavarian community known as Oberammergau. To show their gratitude, the residents made a vow to perform the Passion Play every 10 years. They've kept the promise, and in the process have turned their tiny community into a major stop on the European tourist circuit every 10 years. The play itself runs seven hours, and everybody in the cast, which numbers nearly 2000, is a resident of Oberammergau. It's not the Royal Shakespeare Company, but tickets are tough to come by. You have to write at least a year or two in advance. The next scheduled performance is in 1980. Prices should average around $20.

THE BAYREUTH FESTIVAL

What could be more Wagnerian than Wagner at Bayreuth? Nothing. The season runs about five weeks, from July to late August. If you don't order your tickets at least six months in advance, you might as well stay home. The range is $8 to $54. Most performances begin at 4 P.M.

Hardach Travel Service
500 Fifth Ave.
New York, N.Y. 10017

A NIGHT AT THE GLYNDEBOURNE FESTIVAL OPERA

As if opera weren't civilized enough in its own right: consider the protocol for the performances given by the celebrated opera company whose base is a Tudor estate about two hours' drive from London. Formal dress is obligatory, the way Mozart would have wanted it. You arrive in late afternoon. If you didn't feel like packing a picnic basket of smoked salmon, paté, and wine, you make a reservation at a local restaurant, selecting the wine when you give the order. The performances start at around 5:15, and there is a 75-minute intermission for din-din. You're back in London by midnight. Tickets to the opera run $8.50 (U.S. currency) for upper balcony, and around $23 for center stalls in the orchestra. A box that seats six costs around $128. If you have dinner at the restaurant, figure $50 for two. The season runs from May 31 to August 7. Check your British Tourist Office for details.

234

OPENING NIGHT AT LA SCALA

The opera season at La Scala, in Milan, runs from early December through early June. The best seats cost around $45. For regular performances, figure around $32 for the best orchestra seats.

SHAKESPEARE AT STRATFORD-UPON-AVON

The best of the Bard performed by the Royal Shakespeare Theatre in the Warwickshire town that is, in effect, a shrine to the poet. The annual Shakespeare Festival runs from early April through June. Stay at the Alveston Manor, an Elizabethan house where the first performance of "Midsummer Night's Dream" was given. (There are no room numbers: each room is named after a Shakespearean character.) The top price for the theatre tickets is around £5 ($8.50 in U.S. currency). Figure about £15 for the room. For Saturday night performances, order tickets well in advance.

TWO ORCHESTRA SEATS FOR A HOT BROADWAY SHOW

Regardless of how hot it is, you shouldn't have to pay more than $100 a pair. It's illegal to sell tickets above the printed price—they call it "ice" on Broadway—but if you ask around the ticket agencies and if you look as if you can be trusted, somebody will take care of you.

A BOX AT THE METROPOLITAN OPERA

You have a choice. For an eight-performance package in what they call the Parterre Box—it seats eight—it's $320 a seat. For the five-performance box, it's $200 per seat, with no discount if you buy the entire box. Choice boxes are tough to get. Families keep passing them down from one generation to the next.

BEING WHERE THE ACTION IS

A WEEK AT THE CARIBBEAN'S MOST
EXPENSIVE RESORT

It's in an area of Jamaica called Port Antonio and it's called Frenchman's Cove. The Beatles have slept here. So has Catherine Deneuve. What you get is an ultra-private stone cottage with its own kitchen, a maid to serve you breakfast, and a butler to serve you lunch at the beach and dinner at home. Since it is a healthy walk from the cottages to the little cove beach, they give you a golf cart. The resort sits on 48 acres of hilly beach land. There are a couple of tennis courts, and a boutique owned by one of Errol Flynn's widows. The daily tariff is about $340 per couple, with taxes and tips extra. Your booze is free.

CHRISTMAS AT ST. MORITZ

St. Moritz, and, in particular, the Palace Hotel, is probably the world's most celebrated winter playground, if places of this ilk are to be measured in terms of who stays and plays here. The Shah of Iran has his own villa and is invariably surrounded by a retinue of bodyguards, each of whom appears perfectly capable of dismembering anyone who would deign to maltreat the noble Iranian. The Aga Khan has his own helicopter, the better to avoid the lift lines. All the Greek shipping tycoons ski here, and it's the winter headquarters of Europe's most prominent playboy, Gunther Sachs, who has organized a private club called the Dracula Club. The area is not as old-guard as it used to be, although the Corviglia Club remains one of the world's most exclusive clubs (Eleanor Roosevelt was once refused admission at the door, and King Farouk was blackballed). And profligacy is not as blatant as it was in the good old days when the old Aga Khan reputedly favored the concierge with an advance tip of $10,000 in anticipation of future favors, one of which included a different girl each night. If you stay at the Palace, whose exterior resembles an elaborate storybook cake, you'll have access to the hotel's own staff of ski guides, its private skating rink and bobsled run, and probably the most remarkable indoor swimming pool in the world, replete with bar and waterfalls. An average double room there in high season runs $120 a day European plan. Something in a suite could run as much as $1200 a day, if you can get one, which is unlikely.

A VILLA FOR THE SUMMER IN THE SOUTH OF FRANCE

There are villas and there are villas. A simple house without much of a view might go for around $2000 a month in the summer season. Something more attractive in a private house, with an ocean view and a pool, in a fashionable area like St. Jean Cap Ferrat will probably run you $3000 if you book it through a U.S. real estate agent. Start adding bedrooms and bathrooms and acreage and gardens, and you can easily find a place for $20,000 a month. Household help is generally extra, but the U.S. agent can get help for you at around $600 a month for maids, a little more for a cook. Prices fluctuate according to season and area. St. Tropez, Cannes, and Nice are a little higher than other places, but not necessarily as pretty. From October through May, the rental fees are almost half what they are in high season. In June and September they go about 20% more and in July about 10% more. August is the most expensive month—that's when the Europeans tend to take their vacations. There are options. If you go to France yourself and work through a local real estate agent, you can probably save around 30% to 40% on whatever you finally end up with.

CARNIVAL IN RIO

The bacchanal of all bacchanalia explodes the Friday before Ash Wednesday and runs out of steam on the dawn of the following Wednesday, the beginning of Lent. There are non-stop parties and street dancing and general madness throughout the period, but the Big Event is the all-night samba parade that starts on Sunday night at 8 P.M. and doesn't end until 10 the next morning. Tickets to the parade alone start at $20 and are scalped up to $100. Tickets to the lavish carnival balls that go on almost every night of the celebration run around $50 a person, which includes your dinner. Otherwise, you'll pay normal Brazil prices: about $40 a night for a double at a nice hotel and around $25 for a dinner for two at a nice restaurant. Flying down will be your biggest expense: around $1200.

GOOD SEATS FOR A CHAMPIONSHIP SPORTING EVENT

The trick is not paying for them, it's getting them at the listed price. All tickets for the Super Bowl, for instance, sell for $20, no matter where you sit, but most are gobbled up by corporations and season ticket holders and scalpers who get as much as $100 a seat for a good ticket. The top price for a World Series ticket is around $15, which gets you a box seat. Stanley Cup tickets usually go for around $17 for good seats while basketball playoff seats sell for around a $15 top. If you want a great seat for the Kentucky Derby, you should consult your local clergyman. The two best sections, section N in the Fourth Clubhouse and the third-floor clubhouse box that houses Princess Margaret every year, have waiting lists that will probably exceed your lifetime. For the record, the section N seats run $2400 for 16 seats, but that's for both Friday and Saturday. The third-floor box runs $480 for six seats, both days. The least expensive *seat* at Churchill Downs for Derby Day is $15, which includes the $10 general admission, but you'll have to probably wait a year or two to get one of those, too. Make sure, too, you figure in your hotel room. Nearly all Louisville hotels book only on a three-day basis for the Derby weekend, their prices ranging from $150 to $200 European plan.

SINATRA AT CAESAR'S PALACE

Sinatra doesn't make it to a nightclub stage very often, but when he does it's at Caesar's Palace, and the tariff is $25 a person. Time was when the $25 included your dinner, but things are getting tough even in Vegas. It's now a cocktail show. To get even the minimum, figure about 10 Singapore slings. The line outside is usually very long.

NEW YEAR'S EVE WITH GUY LOMBARDO

Depending upon how close you sit to the bandstand, a seat at a table in the grand ballroom of New York's Waldorf-Astoria Hotel—Guy Lombardo's New Year's Eve hangout for the past 2000 years—fetches between $90 and $125 a person. The price includes a filet mignon dinner, hats, noisemakers, and the opportunity to catch the normal Waldorf-Astoria floorshow.

ODDS AND ENDS

A HOME COMPUTER

To figure out your taxes, keep track of your wines, plan your menus, and play chess with you. The skin and bones basics is a computer processing unit that includes the computer itself and a limited capacity for feeding data in and out. Not very sexy but cheap: $400. To jazz it up, you'll need a keyboard with letters and numbers, around $50, plus a video monitor that can be rigged up with an out-of-service television set and an output printer or teletype. These doodads, along with memory and other programs to run on the machine, will hike the start-up costs to around $3000. Check out electronics stores.

TAPE CASSETTES OF YOUR FAVORITE OLD RADIO SHOWS

Among them: Date With Judy (remember Oogie), The Judy Canova Show, My Friend Irma, Corliss Archer (remember Dexter), The Great Gildersleeve *(Lee*'roy!), Lum and Abner, Duffy's Tavern ("Ah, hello Duffy . . ."), Bob and Ray, Baby Snooks, W. C. Fields, Abbott and Costello, Jack Benny, Amos 'n Andy, Fibber McGee and Molly, Fred Allen, Mr. Keen (tracer of lost persons), The FBI in Peace and War, The Green Hornet, Inner Sanctum (creeeeeeeeeeek), The Shadow Knows, War of the Worlds, The Lone Ranger, Your Hit Parade, etc. Whew. Somebody in Norwalk, Connecticut, has put 100 old-time classic radio programs on standard tape cassettes. The price for each program is $2.98. You get any four for $11.50, and you can buy the whole batch for about $255. Write for a catalogue.

Business Mail Associates
P.O. Box 2189
Norwalk, Ct. 06852

AN OIL PORTRAIT OF YOUR DOG

Don't worry. Nobody expects a dog (or cat) to sit still for hours on end while a temperamental artist works on his portrait. What you do is send in a good photograph. Professionals in the field charge between $300 and $500. Check under Animal Portraits in the *Yellow Pages*.

A TYPEWRITER THAT WRITES IN CHINESE

Among the 145 languages available in the typewriters at Tytell Typewriter is one that writes in Chinese. It operates under a rather complex principle and costs $1500. It sells better in Peking than it does in Peoria.

Tytell Typewriter Co.
116 Fulton St.
New York, N.Y. 10038

A SNOWFLAKE PRESERVATION KIT

Contrary to popular belief, all snowflakes do not look alike. A kit that shows you how to preserve snowflakes and gives you the stuff to preserve it with is $3.95.

Edmund Scientific Co.
555 Edscorp Bldg.
Barrington, N.Y. 08007

A MIRROR THAT TELLS YOU LIES

Some mirrors *do* lie. You can buy a flesh-tint mirror—a pink thing that when you look into it doesn't show up your wrinkles. They have them in convalescent homes. They're not easy to get, but your glass dealer can probably get hold of the glass for around $4 a square foot. Hound him. Mirrors that make you look taller and slimmer are easier to come by. The effect comes about because the glass on the mirror is curved. You can even get a model to slim down just your head. Hammacher

Schlemmer sells it for $895. Normal-size mirrors that make you look skinny sell for around $110. Check with your glass dealer, or with Select-A-Size, a Syracuse company that specializes in these kinds of mirrors.

Select-A-Size
5858 E. Molloy Rd.
Syracuse, N.Y. 13211

GERMAN AIR BY THE HALF-PINT

German air is sold, by the half-pint, in souvenir shops in Berlin. It's called *Berliner luft*. It costs $0.80.

A DOG SLED

The best dog sleds in the country are made by a New Hampshire man named Dick McDonald, who uses only white ash in his sleds. The McDonald is to the sport of world championship dog-sled racing what the name Ferrari is to grand prix car racing. The standard seven-foot racing sled runs $250. A 12-foot freight sled starts at $350. You supply the dogs. McDonald does his building in Laconia, New Hampshire.

A POCKET TELEVISION SET

Granted, you need a reasonably big pocket—one that will accommodate a set that is 4 inches wide, 6 inches long and 1.5 inches deep. But such a television, with a 2-inch screen, has been developed by Sinclair Radionics, in England. It came on the market in 1977. It operates on either batteries or electricity. Around $300.

A MAIL ORDER PhD

Who's gonna know? In Santa Ana, California, there is a "university" called California Western that will set you up with a home study PhD program for around $1700. The requirements, as you might imagine, are hardly onerous. In some cases, you'll have to write a research paper that, according to people investigating the diploma-by-mail industry, may never be read. A book, *College Degrees by Mail,* by John Bear, gives a good description of all the places involved in this academic monkey business.

A POSH KENNEL FOR YOUR DOG

Probably the best you're going to manage is the American Pet Motel in Prairie View, Ill. It's a six-acre spread, and the nicest room in the house is the "Imperial" room, which comes with its own 16-foot patio, a miniature brass bed and mattress, a private water fountain, a red plastic fire hydrant, and piped-in FM music. They change the sheets daily, will serve your dog breakfast in bed, give him two cookie breaks a day, and if you like, will periodically play a taped message supplied by you. The food, unfortunately, isn't exactly haute cuisine—your basic chicken or beef dog food—but they'll honor special diets. The nightly rate is $7, which includes maid service. Tipping is unnecessary.

$10,000 WORTH OF MINCED MONEY

What it is is shredded bread. When U.S. currency gets old, the Treasury Department shreds it. Now some enterprising businessmen are buying it up and packaging it in jars. The standard jar, with about $10,000 of shredded money, sells for $5.

EXOTIC PETS

The exotic pet market is drying up—a victim of government regulations which forbid the exporting and importing of most of the truly unusual pets, and a victim, too, of local zoning regulations that make it difficult to own all but a handful of animals as pets. There are some exceptions. Monkeys are available in certain pet stores around the country. If you want a chimpanzee, figure around $2000—if you can get one. Lion cubs run around $350, but if you don't know what you're doing, you'll have to get rid of it in less than a year. A pet armadillo will run you around $25, but armadillos like to dig and aren't really suited for most home environments. A camel will cost you around $2500. Interested in a nice snake? About $200 will buy you the largest snake in the Western Hemisphere—the anaconda, which when full grown measures between 18 and 25 feet, yet doesn't have that much of an appetite. One of the best exotic pets you can still buy is a llama. Llamas are a domesticated species of the camel family and make terrific pets, really. They will eat just about everything, can go long stretches without water, and are extremely loyal as long as you don't work them too hard. Llamas are used as pack animals in the Andes. A healthy one should run around $500.

Trefflich's Pet Shop
141 W. Broadway
New York, N.Y. 10013

A PINBALL MACHINE

Pinball machines are priced like cars, cost being a matter of model, year, and condition. A used machine in any sort of decent shape is going to run you about $300 to $350. It's basically the same machine you used to play at the corner candy store: five balls, lots of bumping and ringing, with any number of variations to pick from. The top machine in the field today is Fireball, which is what the true pinball connoisseur would choose given his druthers. It should run you around $1000. A new pinball machine—and it's not too smart from a depreciation point of view to buy it new—will run anywhere from $1300, even for the fancy arcade games with the explosions and the other garbage. Antique pinball machines that date back to the 1890's can run into the thousands. The only smart way to buy a pinball machine is to go somewhere that sells them and to keep playing them until you find one you really like.

A PACHINKO MACHINE

Pachinko is a noisy, addictive pinball machine game that is to Japan what slot machines are to Las Vegas. The idea is to flick a ball in a way to make it travel through a maze of obstacles and eventually land inside a certain pocket. When this happens, an inner mechanism springs about 15 new balls, which means the game could theoretically go on forever. Most of the machines sold in the U.S. are reconditioned numbers from Japanese pachinko parlors. Larger stores, like Hammacher Schlemmer, charge around $75 for them. Import outlets generally peddle them for around $60.

A YURT

It's a teepee-like dwelling first developed by the nomads who hang around the plains of Mongolia. It is insulated, simple to build, and portable, and it measures about 16 × 20 feet. Since prices start at $1000, the mortgage payments aren't painful.

Frog Pond Publishers
The Mating
Ridge, N.H. 03461

A LIFESIZE JIGSAW PUZZLE OF YOURSELF

Dressed or undressed, seated or standing, smiling or scowling, flexing a muscle or sticking your tongue out—no matter. Send a large enough negative—preferably 8″ × 10″ but no smaller than 4″ × 5″—to Stave Puzzles in Vermont, and they'll make up a 3,500 piece puzzle of ¼″ plywood. Ideal for the introspective puzzle freak. In black and white, figure around $1200. In color, figure closer to $1500. (It costs about $300 just to blow up the color negative.) Something less ambitious—a 16″ × 20″ with around 200 pieces—should run you around $250. Stave will make a customized wooden puzzle out of virtually any photograph or print you dig up, or you can order from their catalogue. A 375 piece Picasso print (16" × 12") will run around $135. Lautrec's Moulin Rouge poster (975 pieces) is $340. In general, prices run 30¢ a piece.

Stave Puzzles, Inc.
Norwich, Vt. 05055

A ONE-HORSE SLEIGH

The trick is to keep the snow clean-up crews from clearing the streets before you take to the road. Asphalt and jingle bells do not mix. Companies that rent one-horse sleighs—mainly specialty rental companies that service the advertising and entertainment business—generally charge around $50 an hour, which includes the driver, the horse, and the insurance. Check *Yellow Pages.*

YOUR OWN SOUND EFFECTS RECORD

To do with what you will. The selection is infinite: a landslide, bacon frying, a basketball dribbling, a bowling strike, a baby crying, radio static, an electric blender (fast or slow speed), a body falling downstairs, a body falling downstairs, *slow.* A typical sound effects record runs $6 and usually has 35 or so different sounds. Get a catalogue.

Thomas J. Valentino, Inc.
151 W. 46th St.
New York, N.Y. 10036